Fire and

A Journey Through Iceland's Natural Wonders

By: Dane Joe

Contents.

My Personal Experience in Iceland

Iceland is a country that has always fascinated me with its natural beauty, rich culture, and friendly people. That is why I decided to visit it for a vacation in early June 2023. I stayed there for one month, and it was one of the most memorable experiences of my life.

One of the things that I enjoyed the most was visiting the museums in Iceland. I learned a lot about the history, art, and literature of this Nordic nation. I was especially impressed by the National Museum of Iceland, which showcases the heritage and identity of the Icelandic people from the settlement to the present day. I also visited the Reykjavik Art Museum, which displays the works of contemporary Icelandic artists. I admired the creativity and diversity of their expressions.

Another thing that I enjoyed was exploring the natural wonders of Iceland. I was amazed by the geysers, waterfalls, volcanoes, glaciers, and hot springs that dot the landscape. I took a tour of the Golden Circle, which covers some of the most iconic attractions such as Thingvellir National Park, Geysir, and Gullfoss. I also went to the Blue Lagoon, which is a geothermal spa that offers relaxation and healing. I felt refreshed and rejuvenated after soaking in the mineral-rich water.

However, my trip was not without challenges or difficulties. One of the main challenges was the language barrier. Although most Icelanders speak English, I sometimes had trouble understanding their accent or expressions. I also wanted to learn some Icelandic words and phrases, but I found it hard to pronounce them correctly. I had to use a lot of gestures and body language to communicate with the locals.

Another challenge was the weather. Iceland is known for its unpredictable and harsh weather conditions. It can change from sunny to rainy to snowy in a matter of minutes. I had to pack clothes for all seasons and be prepared for any situation. I also had to adjust to the long daylight hours in the summer. It was hard to sleep when the sun was still shining at midnight.

Despite these challenges, I learned a lot from my experience in Iceland. I learned to be more open-minded and curious about different cultures and perspectives. I learned to appreciate the beauty and diversity of nature and how to protect it. I learned to be more flexible and adaptable to changing circumstances and environments. I learned to be more grateful and humble for what I have and what I can do.

In conclusion, my personal experience in Iceland was a wonderful and enriching one. I enjoyed every moment of it and gained so many things. I would love to visit Iceland again and discover more of its secrets and charms.

What to expect.

1. Introduction to Iceland:
   - Explore Iceland's captivating landscapes, from glaciers to geysers.
   - Uncover the allure of a country steeped in Norse mythology and folklore.

2. Planning Your Trip:
   - Navigate the seasons: Winter's Northern Lights or summer's Midnight Sun?
   - Demystify visa requirements and practical travel considerations.

3. Top Destinations and Landmarks:
   - Reykjavik: Modern city with a Viking past.
   - Golden Circle: Geysers, waterfalls, and historical sites.
   - Jökulsárlón Glacier Lagoon: Witness the dance of icebergs.

4. Outdoor Adventures:
   - Hike to hidden waterfalls and volcanic landscapes.
   - Soak in hot springs like the locals or venture into ice caves.

5. Cuisine and Dining:
   - Sample Icelandic delicacies: fermented shark and lamb stew.
   - Sip on local craft beers and experience Nordic culinary trends.

6. Cultural Experiences:
   - Dive into local festivals and traditions.
   - Connect with the artistic vibe in Reykjavik's vibrant arts scene.

7. Practical Tips:
   - Traverse the Ring Road by car or explore public transportation.
   - Choose accommodations, whether it's a cozy guesthouse or a luxury hotel.
   - Stay safe with weather-appropriate gear and local safety guidelines.

8. Activities and Excursions:
   - Chase the Northern Lights or embark on a whale-watching adventure.
   - Experience the thrill of a snowmobile tour on a glacier.

9. Packing Guide:
   - Prepare for Iceland's ever-changing weather with layering essentials.
   - Pack for specific seasons: thermal wear for winter or waterproof gear for rain.

10. Photography and Souvenirs:
    - Capture the essence of Iceland with photography tips.
    - Bring home unique souvenirs like handmade woolens and volcanic rock crafts.

11. Important websites to find and see more
12. Language Guide.

Before diving into the travel guide, let's give you common language tips.

Basic Greetings:
1. Hello - Halló (HAL-loh)
2. Good morning - Góðan dag (GOTH-an dag)
3. Good afternoon - Góðan daginn (GOTH-an THAH-yin)

4. Good evening - Góðan kvöld (GOTH-an kvuth)
5. Good night - Góða nótt (GOTH-a noht)

Common Phrases:
6. Please - Vinsamlegast (VIN-sam-leh-gast)
7. Thank you - Takk (tahk)
8. You're welcome - Þú ert velkominn (thoo ert VEL-koh-meen)
9. Excuse me - Afsakið (AF-sa-kith)
10. I'm sorry - Ég er leiður (yeh er LAY-thur)

Polite Expressions:
11. Yes - Já (yow)
12. No - Nei (nay)
13. May I? / Can I? - Má ég? (ma yeh)
14. Could you help me, please? - Gætirðu að hjálpa mér, vinsamlegast? (gai-thir-thoo ath HYOWL-pa mayr, VIN-sam-leh-gast)

Getting Around:
15. Where is...? - Hvar er...? (kvar air...?)
16. How do I get to...? - Hvernig kem ég til...? (kver-nik kem yay til...?)
17. Bus station - Umferðarmiðstöð (UM-fer-thar-mith-stuth)

18. Train station - Lestarstöð (LEH-star-stuth)

Numbers:
19. Zero - Núll (nool)
20. One - Eitt (ayt)
21. Two - Tvö (tvoe)
22. Three - Þrjú (three-yu)
23. Four - Fjórir (FYOR-ir)
24. Five - Fimm (feem)
25. Ten - Tíu (tee-oo)
26. Twenty - Tuttugu (TOOT-too)

Time and Dates:
27. What time is it? - Hvað er klukkan? (kvaeth er KLOH-kun?)
28. Today - Í dag (ee thahg)
29. Tomorrow - Á morgun (ow MOR-gun)
30. Yesterday - Í gær (ee gai-r)

Directions:
31. North - Norður (NORTH-ur)
32. South - Suður (SU-thur)
33. East - Austur (OW-stur)
34. West - Vestur (VES-tur)

Dining Out:

35. Menu - Matseðill (mat-SE-thil)

36. Water - Vatn (vathn)

37. Coffee - Kaffi (ka-fi)

38. Delicious - Góður (GOTH-ur)

Shopping and Transactions:

39. How much is this? - Hvað kostar þetta? (kvað kost-ar thet-ta?)

40. I would like to buy... - Ég vil kaupa... (yeh vil KOW-pa...)

41. Can I pay by credit card? - Get ég borgað með greiðslukorti? (get yeh BOR-gath meth GRAYTH-sluh-kor-tee?)

Accommodations:

42. Hotel - Hótel (HOH-tel)

43. Room - Herbergi (HER-ber-gi)

44. Reservation - Bókun (BOH-kun)

45. Key - Lykill (LITL)

Emergency Phrases:

46. Help! - Hjálp! (hyawlp)

47. Fire - Eldur (EL-dur)

48. Police - Lögregla (LUR-gre-glur)

49. Hospital - Sjúkrahús (SYOOK-ra-hoos)
50. Emergency - Neyð (nayth)

This comprehensive guide should help travelers communicate effectively during their Icelandic adventure. Remember to embrace the language, and locals will appreciate your effort!

1. Introduction to Iceland:

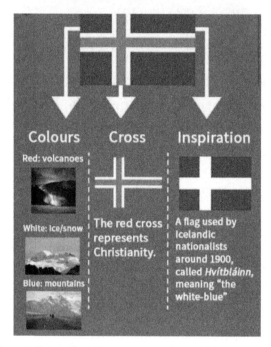

Overview of Iceland's geography, climate, and unique characteristics.

Iceland is a small island country in the North Atlantic Ocean, with a population of about 380,000 people. It is one of the most geologically active and diverse places on Earth, with volcanoes, glaciers, geysers, waterfalls, and hot springs. It is also one of the most developed and progressive countries in the world, with a high standard of living and a strong democracy.

Iceland has a long and rich history, dating back to the Viking age of exploration and settlement. The Icelandic people have a unique culture and identity, shaped by their isolation and interaction with nature. They are known for their storytelling and literature, especially the Icelandic sagas, which are among the finest literary achievements of the Middle Ages. They also have a vibrant music and art scene, as well as a passion for outdoor sports and adventure.

Iceland is a country that offers many attractions and experiences for visitors. It is a place where one can witness the beauty and power of nature, from the Northern Lights to the erupting volcanoes. It is a place where one can learn about the history and culture of a people who have survived and thrived in a harsh environment. It is a place where one can enjoy the warmth and hospitality of the locals, who are friendly and welcoming.

Iceland is a country that has something for everyone, whether one is looking for relaxation, education, or excitement. It is a country that is worth exploring and discovering, as it has many secrets and charms. It is a country that will leave a lasting impression on anyone who visits it.

Brief history and cultural background.

-Introduction

Iceland is a Nordic island country located in the North Atlantic Ocean, between North America and Europe. It has a population of about 380,000 people and a land area of 103,125 square kilometers. It is one of the most sparsely populated and geologically active countries in the world, with many volcanoes, geysers, hot springs, glaciers, and lava fields. Iceland is also known for its rich cultural heritage, which includes the Icelandic sagas, the oldest preserved literary works in Europe, and the Althing, the oldest parliament in the world[1].

Iceland's history can be divided into several periods, from its early settlement by Norse and Celtic people in the 9th and 10th centuries, to its integration into Norway and Denmark in the Middle Ages, to its struggle for independence and sovereignty in the 19th and 20th centuries, to its modern development as a prosperous and progressive nation in the 21st century. In this essay, I will explore the main events, achievements, and challenges that shaped Iceland's history and identity.

- *Early Settlement and Commonwealth (874-1262)*

The first permanent settlers of Iceland were Norse and Celtic (Scottish and Irish) immigrants who arrived in the late 9th and early 10th centuries. According to the Landnámabók (Book of Settlements), a medieval source that records the names and origins of the settlers, the first settler was Ingólfur Arnarson, who claimed Reykjavik as his land in 874[2]. The settlers came mostly from Norway, where they were fleeing the centralization and tyranny of King Harald Fairhair, who unified the country under his rule. Some of the settlers also brought slaves and concubines from the British Isles, who contributed to the genetic and cultural diversity of the population[3].

The settlers established a commonwealth based on a system of laws and assemblies, without a central authority or a king. The main legislative and judicial body was the Althing, which was founded in 930 at Thingvellir, a plain near Reykjavik. The Althing was composed of 36 chieftains (goðar) and their representatives, who met annually to enact laws, settle disputes, and elect a lawspeaker, who recited the laws from memory. The Althing also served as a forum for social and religious activities, such as trade, marriage, and sacrifice[4].

The settlers also developed a rich literary and artistic tradition, which is best exemplified by the Icelandic sagas, prose narratives that recount the lives and deeds of the settlers and their descendants. The sagas are considered among the finest literary achievements of the Middle Ages, as they depict realistic characters, complex plots, and vivid descriptions of the natural and social environment. The sagas also reflect a European outlook, as they often refer to historical events and figures in Norway, England, France, and other countries. Some of the most famous sagas are Njáls saga, Egils saga, Laxdœla saga, and Grettis saga.

The commonwealth period was also marked by internal conflicts and violence, as the chieftains competed for power and influence, and feuds and bloodshed were common. The most notorious episode was the Sturlungaöld (Age of the Sturlungs), a civil war that lasted from 1220 to 1264, and involved the Sturlung clan and its allies against other rival clans. The civil war weakened the commonwealth and made it vulnerable to foreign intervention.

- *Norwegian and Danish Rule (1262-1918)*

In 1262, Iceland entered into a union with Norway, under the terms of the Old Covenant (Gamli sáttmáli), which recognized the sovereignty of the Norwegian king, but granted Iceland some autonomy and privileges, such as the continuation of the Althing and the preservation of the laws. The union was motivated by the desire of the Icelanders to end the civil war and secure peace and stability, and by the ambition of the Norwegian king to expand his domain and influence. The union also brought some benefits to Iceland, such as trade, education, and ecclesiastical reform.

In 1380, Norway and Iceland came under the rule of Denmark, as a result of the Kalmar Union, which united the Scandinavian kingdoms under a single monarch. The union lasted until 1814, when Norway was ceded to Sweden, while Iceland remained under Danish control. The union had a negative impact on Iceland, as it suffered from economic decline, political oppression, and natural disasters. The trade monopoly, which restricted Iceland's trade to Danish merchants, caused poverty and famine. The Reformation, which was imposed by the Danish king in 1536, abolished the Catholic Church and confiscated its lands and properties. The natural calamities, such as volcanic eruptions, earthquakes, and epidemics, reduced the population and devastated the land.

Despite the hardships, Iceland also experienced some cultural and intellectual revival, especially in the 17th and 18th centuries. The most notable figure was Hallgrímur Pétursson, a Lutheran pastor and poet, who composed the Passion Hymns, a collection of 50 religious poems that express the suffering and redemption of Christ and the Christian faith. The Passion Hymns are regarded as the most influential and popular work of Icelandic literature, and are still sung and recited today. Another prominent figure was Jónas Hallgrímsson, a poet and naturalist, who was one of the founders of the Icelandic nationalist movement, which aimed to restore Iceland's language, culture, and autonomy.

The 19th century saw the rise of the Icelandic independence movement, which was inspired by the ideals of the French and American revolutions, and the Romantic and Nationalist movements in Europe. The movement was led by Jón Sigurðsson, a scholar and politician, who is considered the father of the nation. Jón Sigurðsson advocated for the restoration of the Althing as a representative assembly, the abolition of the trade monopoly, and the recognition of Iceland as a sovereign state within a personal union with Denmark. He also promoted the study and preservation of the Icelandic sagas, the revival of the national dress, and the celebration of the national day on June 17, his birthday.

The movement achieved some success, as Denmark gradually granted Iceland more rights and autonomy, such as the establishment of a constitution, a cabinet, and a flag. However, the full independence of Iceland was delayed by the First World War and the Danish refusal to relinquish its sovereignty. The final push for independence came after the Second World War, when Iceland was occupied by British and American forces, and Denmark was invaded by Nazi Germany. Iceland declared itself a republic on June 17, 1944, and was recognized by Denmark and other countries.

- *Republic and Modernization (1944-present)*

The republic of Iceland faced many challenges and opportunities in the second half of the 20th century, as it underwent rapid economic, social, and political changes. The main factors that contributed to the modernization of Iceland were the Marshall Plan, which provided financial aid and technical assistance from the United States; the NATO membership, which ensured Iceland's security and defense; the fishing industry, which was the main source of income and export; and the welfare state, which provided universal health care, education, and social services.

Iceland also experienced some conflicts and crises, such as the Cod Wars, a series of disputes with the United Kingdom over the fishing rights and boundaries in the North Atlantic; the 1973 volcanic eruption of Eldfell, which destroyed part of the town of Vestmannaeyjar and threatened its inhabitants; the 1975-1985 Women's Strike, which demonstrated the gender inequality and demanded more rights and representation for women; and the 2008-2011 financial crisis, which caused the collapse of the banking system and the devaluation of the currency.

Iceland has also achieved some remarkable accomplishments and innovations, such as the development of renewable energy, which accounts for almost all of the electricity and heating production from hydropower and geothermal sources; the advancement of digital technology, which has made Iceland a leader in internet penetration, e-government, and start-up scene; the promotion of human rights, which has made Iceland one of the most egalitarian and progressive countries in the world, with a strong emphasis on gender equality, LGBTQ+ rights, and environmental protection; and the flourishing of culture and tourism, which has attracted millions of visitors and showcased Iceland's natural beauty, artistic diversity, and social innovation.

- Conclusion

Iceland is a unique and fascinating country that has a long and rich history, from its early settlement by Norse and Celtic people, to its integration into Norway and Denmark, to its struggle for independence and sovereignty, to its modern development as a prosperous and progressive nation. Iceland's history is marked by contrasts and challenges, as well as achievements and opportunities. Iceland is a country that inspires curiosity, creativity, and cooperation, and that has a lot to offer and learn from the world.

Source: (1) Iceland | History, Maps, Flag, Population, Climate, & Facts. https://www.britannica.com/place/Iceland.

(2) A Complete History of Iceland | Guide to Iceland. https://guidetoiceland.is/history-culture/history-of-iceland.

(3) Iceland - The World Factbook.
https://www.cia.gov/the-world-factbook/countries/iceland/.

(4) Iceland History: Origin of Iceland (Maps, Population, Flag).
https://www.iceland.org/culture/history/.

2. Planning Your Trip:

Best times to visit considering weather and seasonal attractions.

Iceland's diverse climate and unique seasonal attractions offer distinct experiences throughout the year, making it a year-round destination for travelers. Understanding the best times to visit depends on your preferences and the type of activities you want to engage in.

1. Summer (June-August):

   - Weather: Iceland experiences milder temperatures during summer, ranging from 50°F to

60°F (10°C to 15°C). Days are long, with almost continuous daylight in June.

   - Attractions: Summer is ideal for exploring the iconic Golden Circle, witnessing stunning waterfalls like Gullfoss, and enjoying outdoor activities like hiking and camping. The highland roads are open, providing access to remote areas.

2. Fall (September-November):

   - Weather: As fall progresses, temperatures begin to drop, ranging from 40°F to 50°F (5°C to 10°C). Days become shorter, but fall colors enhance the landscape.

   - Attractions: This season is perfect for witnessing the Northern Lights, as darkness returns. Explore less crowded sites like the East Fjords and experience local harvest festivals.

3. Winter (December-February):

   - Weather: Winter brings colder temperatures, ranging from 20°F to 30°F (-5°C to -1°C). Days are short, but the snowy landscapes create a magical atmosphere.
   - Attractions: Witness the mesmerizing Northern Lights dance across the sky. Engage in winter sports like ice caving, snowmobiling, and relaxing in geothermal pools. The Blue Lagoon is a unique experience in the winter chill.

4. Spring (March-May):

- Weather: Spring sees a gradual increase in temperatures, ranging from 30°F to 40°F (-1°C to 5°C). Days lengthen, and nature begins to awaken.

- Attractions: Spring is an excellent time for birdwatching, with puffins returning to nesting sites. The melting snow reveals vibrant landscapes, and waterfalls are at their peak. Explore the Reykjanes Peninsula and enjoy the tranquility before the summer crowds arrive.

Considerations:

- Crowds: Summer attracts the most visitors, while winter offers a quieter experience. Spring and fall provide a balance with fewer tourists.

- Road Conditions: Some remote areas are accessible only in summer, while winter may limit access to certain regions. Check road conditions before planning.

Ultimately, the best time to visit Iceland depends on your interests, whether you seek the vibrant energy of summer or the serene beauty of winter's icy landscapes. Each season offers a unique perspective on this enchanting island.

Visa and entry requirements for international travelers.

Iceland, renowned for its stunning landscapes and vibrant culture, has specific visa and entry requirements for international travelers. Understanding these regulations is crucial to ensure a smooth and hassle-free visit.

1. Schengen Area Membership:
   - Iceland is a member of the Schengen Area, a zone comprising 27 European countries that have abolished passport control at their mutual borders. Travelers holding a Schengen visa can enter Iceland without the need for a separate Icelandic visa.

2. Visa Exemptions:

   - Citizens of many countries, including the United States, Canada, Australia, and most European nations, do not require a visa for short stays (up to 90 days within a 180-day period) for tourism, business, or family visits.

3. Visa Application Process:

   - Travelers from countries requiring a visa must apply at an Icelandic embassy or consulate in their home country. The application process typically includes providing a completed application form, passport-sized photos, proof of travel insurance, flight itinerary, accommodation details, and evidence of financial means.

4. Visa Types:

   - Iceland issues different types of visas, including tourist visas, business visas, and visas for family reunification. The type of visa required depends on the purpose of the visit.

5. Passport Requirements:

   - Travelers need a passport valid for at least three months beyond the intended departure date from the Schengen Area. Ensure your passport has at least two blank pages for visa stamps.

6. Residence Permits:
   - Visitors planning to stay in Iceland for more than 90 days or for purposes other than tourism may need a residence permit. This includes individuals seeking employment, students, and those joining family members.

7. Health Insurance:
   - While not mandatory, having travel health insurance is advisable. It ensures coverage for medical expenses in case of illness or accidents during the stay in Iceland.

8. Customs and Border Control:
   - Upon arrival, travelers must clear customs and border control. Be prepared to present relevant documents, including a valid visa, proof of accommodation, and return flight details. Customs regulations prohibit certain items, and travelers should be aware of these restrictions.

9. COVID-19 Requirements:

- Due to the ongoing global pandemic, additional health and safety measures may be in place. Travelers should check for the latest COVID-19 entry requirements, such as testing and quarantine rules.

10. Changes and Updates:
- Visa and entry requirements can change, and it is essential for travelers to stay informed about any updates. Check with official government websites or contact the nearest Icelandic embassy or consulate for the latest information.

In conclusion, while Iceland offers a warm welcome to international travelers, understanding and complying with visa and entry requirements is vital for a seamless and enjoyable visit. Thorough preparation ensures that visitors can fully appreciate the beauty and hospitality that Iceland has to offer.

Currency, language, and essential travel tips.

Iceland is a fascinating country with stunning natural beauty, rich culture, and friendly people. If you are planning to visit Iceland, there are some things you should know about its currency, language, and essential travel tips to make your trip more enjoyable and hassle-free.

-Currency

The official currency in Iceland is the Icelandic Krona (ISK). It is one of the strongest currencies in the world, which means that Iceland is a relatively expensive country to visit for most travelers. The exchange rate of the Icelandic Krona varies depending on the market, but you can check the current rate [here](^1^).

Icelanders rarely use cash and prefer to pay with credit or debit cards for everything, even small purchases. Most places accept major cards such as Visa, Mastercard, and American Express, but it is always a good idea to have some cash on hand for emergencies or tips. You can withdraw cash from ATMs, which are widely available in cities and towns, or exchange money at banks or currency exchange offices. However, be aware that some ATMs may charge fees or have withdrawal limits, and some exchange offices may offer unfavorable rates or commissions.

You can also use foreign currencies such as US dollars, Canadian dollars, and Euros in some tourist hotspots, such as hotels, restaurants, and souvenir shops. However, you may not get the best value for your money, as the exchange rates may be higher than the official ones, and you may not get any change back in your own currency.

- Language

The official language in Iceland is Icelandic, a North Germanic language that is closely related to Norwegian and Faroese. Icelandic is spoken by almost all Icelanders and is considered an important part of their national identity and culture. Icelandic is also one of the oldest and most complex languages in the world, with a rich vocabulary, grammar, and pronunciation that can be challenging for foreigners to learn.

However, you do not need to worry too much about the language barrier, as most Icelanders speak

English very well, especially the younger generations and those who work in the tourism industry. You can communicate with them easily and ask for directions, information, or help. You may also encounter some people who speak other languages, such as Danish, German, French, or Spanish, as Icelanders are generally well-educated and multilingual.

Nevertheless, it is always nice and respectful to learn some basic words and phrases in Icelandic before you go, such as greetings, thank you, please, and numbers. You will impress the locals and make them feel more welcome and friendly towards you. You can also use online tools or apps to help you with the pronunciation and translation of Icelandic words and sentences.

- *Essential travel tips*

Iceland is a wonderful destination for travelers who love nature, adventure, and culture. However, it is also a country with some unique features and challenges that you should be aware of and prepared for. Here are some essential travel tips for your Icelandic adventure:

- Plan your itinerary well. Iceland has a lot to offer, from the famous Golden Circle, Ring Road, and Diamond Circle routes, to the hidden gems and off-the-beaten-path locations. You should decide what you want to see and do, how much time you have, and what mode of transportation you will use. You should also book your accommodation and tours in advance, as they can get sold out quickly, especially during the peak season. You can use online resources or guides to help you plan your trip, or consult with local experts or agencies for customized advice and recommendations.

- Pack smart. Iceland's weather is unpredictable and can change quickly, from sunny and warm to rainy and cold, or even snowy and stormy. You should pack layers of clothing that are suitable for different weather conditions and activities, such as waterproof jackets, warm sweaters, thermal underwear, hats, gloves, scarves, and boots. You should also bring a swimsuit, as Iceland has many natural hot springs and geothermal pools that you can enjoy. You may also need some special equipment or gear, such as sunglasses, sunscreen, hiking shoes, sleeping bags, or tents, depending on your itinerary and preferences.

- Respect nature and culture. Iceland is a country with a fragile and diverse ecosystem, a rich and proud history, and a vibrant and creative society. You should respect and appreciate its nature and culture, and follow the rules and regulations that are in place to protect and preserve them. You should not litter, damage, or disturb the wildlife, plants, or landscapes, and you should stay on the marked trails and roads. You should also not touch, move, or take any rocks, stones, or lava, as they are considered sacred and part of the Icelandic folklore and mythology. You should also learn about and respect the customs, traditions, and beliefs of the Icelandic people, and avoid any actions or words that may offend or insult them. You should also try to experience and enjoy some of the local cuisine, music, art, and literature, and interact with the locals in a friendly and polite manner..

Source: (1) 7 Helpful Things To Know About Money In Iceland.

https://icelandtrippers.com/currency-money-in-iceland/.

(2) Essential Travel Tips for Your Icelandic Adventure.
https://www.gocarrental.is/guides/first-step/iceland-travel-tips/.

(3) Travel Tips Iceland for planning and on the go - Rough Guides.
https://www.roughguides.com/iceland/travel-advice/.

(4) Visas, money and must dos – a first timer's guide to Iceland - Contiki.
https://www.contiki.com/six-two/article/iceland-travel-guide/.

(5) Iceland Currency: What to Know For Your Trip | I am Reykjavik.
https://www.iamreykjavik.com/iceland-currency-exchange-rate-money.

(6) Getty Images.
https://www.gettyimages.com/detail/photo/reykjavik

-capital-city-of-iceland-royalty-free-image/8254284
82.

3. Top Destinations and Landmarks:

Detailed information on must-visit places like Reykjavik, Golden Circle, and Jökulsárlón Glacier Lagoon.

Iceland is a beautiful country with many attractions and activities for travelers of all kinds. Whether you are looking for natural wonders, cultural experiences, or adventure, you will find something to suit your taste in Iceland. Here are some of the most popular and must-visit places in Iceland, [1] [2] [3]:

- Reykjavik:

The capital and largest city of Iceland, Reykjavik is a vibrant and cosmopolitan place with many landmarks, museums, restaurants, and nightlife options. You can visit the iconic Hallgrimskirkja church, the Harpa concert hall, the Perlan museum, and the Sun Voyager sculpture. You can also enjoy whale and puffin watching tours, thermal pools, and street art. Reykjavik is also a great base for exploring the nearby attractions, such as the Golden Circle and the South Coast.

- The Golden Circle:

The Golden Circle is a popular sightseeing route that covers three of the most famous attractions in Iceland: Thingvellir National Park, Geysir Geothermal Area, and Gullfoss waterfall. Thingvellir is a UNESCO

World Heritage Site where you can see the rift between the North American and Eurasian tectonic plates, and the site of the first Icelandic parliament. Geysir is a geothermal area where you can witness the eruptions of hot springs, especially the Strokkur geyser. Gullfoss is a majestic waterfall that plunges into a canyon with a rainbow often visible on sunny days. You can also visit other attractions along the way, such as the Kerid crater lake, the Faxi waterfall, and the Fridheimar greenhouse.

- The Blue Lagoon:

The Blue Lagoon is one of the most famous and visited attractions in Iceland. It is a geothermal spa that offers a relaxing and rejuvenating experience in mineral-rich waters that are said to have healing properties for the skin. The water is a stunning turquoise color and the temperature is around 38°C (100°F). You can also enjoy other facilities, such as saunas, steam rooms, massages, and a restaurant. The Blue Lagoon is located on the Reykjanes Peninsula, near the Keflavik International Airport, and you can book your tickets in advance online.

- The South Coast:

The South Coast is a scenic route that showcases some of the most diverse and spectacular landscapes in Iceland. You can see waterfalls, volcanoes, glaciers, black sand beaches, and more. Some of the highlights include the Seljalandsfoss and Skogafoss waterfalls, the Eyjafjallajokull and Katla volcanoes, the

Solheimajokull and Vatnajokull glaciers, the Reynisfjara and Vik black sand beaches, the Dyrholaey and Reynisdrangar rock formations, and the Jokulsarlon glacier lagoon and Diamond Beach. You can also visit the Skaftafell Nature Reserve, where you can hike to the Svartifoss waterfall and the Skaftafellsjokull glacier tongue.

- The Westfjords:

The Westfjords are a remote and rugged region in the northwest of Iceland, where you can experience the wild and unspoiled nature of the country. You can explore the dramatic fjords, cliffs, mountains, and valleys, and see abundant wildlife, such as seals, whales, birds, and arctic foxes. You can also visit the Hornstrandir Nature Reserve, where you can hike and camp in the wilderness, the Latrabjarg bird cliffs, where you can see puffins and other seabirds, the Dynjandi waterfall, where you can admire the cascading tiers of water, and the Raudisandur beach, where you can enjoy the golden-red sand and the views of the sea.

- The Snaefellsnes Peninsula:

The Snaefellsnes Peninsula is a small but diverse region in the west of Iceland, where you can see many natural and cultural attractions. You can visit the Snaefellsjokull National Park, where you can see the Snaefellsjokull glacier and volcano, which inspired the novel Journey to the Center of the Earth by Jules Verne. You can also visit the Kirkjufell mountain and waterfall, which are among the most photographed spots in Iceland, the Arnarstapi and Hellnar fishing villages, where you can see the basalt columns and arches, the Djupalonssandur and Skardsvik beaches, where you can see the black and white sand and the shipwreck remains, and the Stykkisholmur town, where you can see the colorful houses and the Norwegian heritage museum.

- The Eastfjords:

The Eastfjords are a region in the east of Iceland, where you can enjoy the scenic and tranquil fjords, mountains, and coastlines. You can visit the Seydisfjordur town, where you can see the rainbow street and the sound sculpture Tvísöngur, the

Egilsstadir town, where you can see the Lagarfljot lake and the Hallormsstadur forest, the Djupivogur town, where you can see the Eggs of Merry Bay sculpture and the Papey island, and the Stodvarfjordur town, where you can see the Petra's Stone Collection museum. You can also visit the Borgarfjordur Eystri town, where you can see the puffin colony and the Elf Garden, and the Faskrudsfjordur town, where you can see the French heritage museum and the Northern Lights Observatory.

- The North:

The North is a region in the north of Iceland, where you can see some of the most impressive and diverse attractions in the country. You can visit the Akureyri town, where you can see the botanical garden, the art museum, and the Christmas house, the Husavik town, where you can see the whale museum and the whale watching tours, the Myvatn area, where you can see the volcanic craters, lava fields, hot springs, and the Myvatn Nature Baths, and the Dettifoss waterfall, where you can see the most powerful waterfall in Europe. You can also visit the Godafoss waterfall, where you can see the waterfall of the gods, the Asbyrgi canyon, where you can see the horseshoe-shaped canyon and the Eyjan pond, and the Hverir geothermal area, where you can see the boiling mud pools and fumaroles.

- The Highlands:

The Highlands are a region in the interior of Iceland, where you can see the most remote and rugged landscapes in the country. You can visit the Landmannalaugar area, where you can see the colorful rhyolite mountains, the Laugavegur hiking trail, and the natural hot springs, the Thorsmork valley, where you can see the glacial rivers, birch forests, and the Eyjafjallajokull volcano, the Kerlingarfjoll area, where you can see the geothermal activity, the snow-capped peaks, and the Kverkfjoll ice caves, and the Askja caldera, where you can see the Viti crater lake and the Holuhraun lava field. You can also visit the Laki craters, where you can see the largest volcanic eruption in recorded history, the Eldgja canyon, where you can see the largest volcanic canyon in the world, and the Hveravellir geothermal area, where you can see the hot springs, geysers, and the Kjalhraun lava field.

- The Westman Islands:

The Westman Islands are a group of islands in the south of Iceland, where you can see the volcanic and cultural history of the country. You can visit the Heimaey island, where you can see the Eldfell volcano, which erupted in 1973 and buried part of the town, the Eldheimar museum, which displays the remains of the houses and the stories of the eruption, the Storhofdi lighthouse, which offers a panoramic view of the islands and the puffins, and the Sagnheimar museum, which displays the history and culture of the islands. You can also visit Surtsey island, which was formed by a volcanic eruption in 1963 and is a UNESCO World Heritage Site and a natural laboratory for studying the colonization of new land by plants and animals.

I hope this information helps you to plan your trip to Iceland and enjoy its amazing attractions. Have a great time! ●

Source:
 (1) 18 Things To Do & Places to Visit In Iceland - Guide to Iceland.
https://guidetoiceland.is/nature-info/what-to-do-in-iceland.

(2) 12 best places to visit in Iceland - Lonely Planet.
https://www.lonelyplanet.com/articles/best-places-to-visit-in-iceland.

(3) Top 10 - Ten must-visit places in Iceland - Introducing Iceland.
https://www.introducingiceland.com/top-ten.

Historical significance and cultural insights about each destination.

Each destination in Iceland has its own historical significance and cultural insights that can enrich your travel experience. Here are some brief summaries of each destination.[1][2][3]:

- Reykjavik: Reykjavik is the oldest permanent settlement in Iceland, dating back to the 9th century. It was the site of the first Althing, the national parliament, in 930 AD. Reykjavik is also the cultural and artistic center of Iceland, hosting many festivals, events, and exhibitions throughout the year. Reykjavik is known for its colorful houses, quirky museums, and creative atmosphere.

- The Golden Circle: The Golden Circle is a historical and geological wonderland, where you can witness the natural forces that shaped Iceland's landscape and history. Thingvellir is the birthplace of Icelandic democracy and the place where the continental drift is visible. Geysir is the origin of the word geyser and the home of the most active geyser in Iceland, Strokkur. Gullfoss is a spectacular waterfall that symbolizes the power and beauty of nature.

- The Blue Lagoon: The Blue Lagoon is a modern marvel of geothermal engineering and spa therapy. It was created in 1976 by accident, when runoff water from a geothermal power plant formed a pool in a lava field. The water was discovered to have beneficial effects on the skin, especially for psoriasis patients. The Blue Lagoon is now one of the most popular attractions in Iceland, offering a relaxing and rejuvenating experience in a stunning setting.

- The South Coast: The South Coast is a showcase of Iceland's diverse and dramatic scenery, from waterfalls and volcanoes to glaciers and beaches. The South Coast is also rich in history and folklore, as many of the sites are associated with sagas, legends, and myths. For example, Eyjafjallajokull is the volcano that erupted in 2010 and caused a global disruption of air travel. Reynisfjara is the black sand beach that features basalt columns and sea stacks that are said to be trolls turned to stone by the sun.

- The Westfjords: The Westfjords are a remote and rugged region that offers a glimpse into the traditional and authentic Icelandic way of life. The Westfjords are the oldest part of Iceland, dating back to the Ice Age. They are also the least populated and most isolated part of the country, with only a few small towns and villages. The Westfjords are known for their wildlife, especially seals, whales, and birds, as well as their natural attractions, such as hot springs, waterfalls, and beaches.

- The Snaefellsnes Peninsula: The Snaefellsnes Peninsula is a miniature version of Iceland, featuring a variety of landscapes and attractions in a small area. The Snaefellsnes Peninsula is also a place of mystery and magic, as it is the setting of the novel Journey to the Center of the Earth by Jules Verne. The Snaefellsjokull glacier and volcano is the entrance to the underground world in the novel, and is also believed to be a source of spiritual energy and a gateway to other dimensions.

- The Eastfjords: The Eastfjords are a region of contrasts, where the mountains meet the sea, and the old meets the new. The Eastfjords are home to some of the oldest and most charming towns in Iceland, as well as some of the most modern and innovative industries, such as fishing, aluminum, and renewable energy. The Eastfjords are also known for their natural beauty, such as lakes, waterfalls, and islands, as well as their cultural heritage, such as stone collections, sculptures, and museums.

- The North: The North is a region of diversity and adventure, where you can find some of the most impressive and varied attractions in Iceland. The North is home to the second largest city in Iceland, Akureyri, which is a hub of culture, education, and entertainment. The North is also home to the Lake Myvatn area, which is one of the most geologically active and ecologically rich areas in the world. The North is also known for its waterfalls, such as Dettifoss and Godafoss, which are among the most powerful and beautiful in Europe.

- The Highlands: The Highlands are a region of wilderness and exploration, where you can experience the most remote and untouched parts of Iceland. The Highlands are only accessible by 4x4 vehicles or on foot, and only during the summer months, when the roads and trails are open. The Highlands are a paradise for hikers, campers, and adventurers, who can enjoy the stunning scenery of mountains, glaciers, volcanoes, and hot springs. The Highlands are also a place of history and culture, as many of the sites are linked to sagas, legends, and events.

- The Westman Islands: The Westman Islands are a group of islands that offer a unique and diverse experience of Iceland. The Westman Islands are the result of volcanic activity, and have a history of eruptions, invasions, and evacuations. The Westman Islands are also home to the largest puffin colony in the world, as well as other seabirds and marine life. The Westman Islands are also known for their culture and festivals, such as the annual Thjodhatid festival, which celebrates the end of the Turkish raids in the 17th century.

I hope this information gives you an overview of the historical significance and cultural insights of each destination in Iceland. If you want to learn more, you can visit the websites of each destination or use the web search tool to find more sources. Have a wonderful trip! ●

Source:
(1) The Top 12 Historical Destinations In Europe You Didn't Know About.
https://theculturetrip.com/europe/articles/top-12-historical-destinations-in-europe-you-didn-t-know-about.

(2) Travels Through Culture: Understanding its Influence on Tourism.
https://brilliantio.com/how-does-culture-affect-travel-and-tourism/.

(3) Historical significance explained - History Skills.
https://www.historyskills.com/historical-knowledge/significance/.

4. Outdoor Adventures:

Recommendations for hiking trails, hot springs, and waterfalls.

Iceland is a paradise for hikers, nature lovers, and adventure seekers. There are many hiking trails, hot springs, and waterfalls to explore and enjoy in this amazing country. Here are some recommendations for you.[1] [2] [3]:

- Hiking trails

- Laugavegur Trail:

This is the most famous trail in Iceland, a 55 km (34 mile) trek across the Icelandic wilderness. You will see polychrome mountains, lava fields, black sand deserts, geothermal springs, glaciers, lakes, icy river-crossings, grassy plains and forests. It takes 4 days to complete and you can camp or stay in huts along the way. The best time to go is from June to September.

- Fimmvörðuháls Trail:

This is a 25 km (16 mile) trail that connects the Laugavegur Trail and the Skógafoss waterfall. You will see two new volcanoes that were formed by the 2010 eruption of Eyjafjallajökull, as well as glaciers, canyons, and waterfalls. It takes 1 to 2 days to complete and you can camp or stay in a hut at the end of the trail. The best time to go is from June to September.

- Reykjadalur Hot Spring Thermal River: This is a 5 km (3 mile) trail that leads to a natural hot spring river where you can soak and relax. You will see geothermal activity, colorful hills, and great views. It takes 2 to 3 hours to complete and you can go all year round, but be prepared for cold weather in winter.

- Snaefellsjökull Glacier:

This is a 15 km (9 mile) trail that takes you to the summit of the Snaefellsjökull glacier and volcano, which inspired the novel Journey to the Center of the Earth by Jules Verne. You will see snow, ice, and stunning views of the ocean and the peninsula. It takes 8 to 10 hours to complete and you need a guide and special equipment. The best time to go is from June to August.

- Kirkjufell Mountain: This is a 3 km (2 mile) trail that takes you to the top of Kirkjufell, the most photographed mountain in Iceland. You will see a steep and rocky ascent, a waterfall, and a panoramic view of the bay and the town. It takes 3 hours to complete and it is a dangerous hike, so it is best to do it with a guide. The best time to go is from May to September.

- *Hot springs*

- The Blue Lagoon: This is the most famous and visited hot spring in Iceland. It is a geothermal spa that offers a relaxing and rejuvenating experience in mineral-rich waters that are said to have healing properties for the skin. The water is a stunning turquoise color and the temperature is around 38°C (100°F). You can also enjoy other facilities, such as saunas, steam rooms, massages, and a restaurant. You need to book your tickets in advance online and the best time to go is early in the morning or late in the evening to avoid the crowds.

- Myvatn Nature Baths:

This is a less crowded and cheaper alternative to the Blue Lagoon. It is a geothermal pool that offers a similar experience in alkaline waters that are good for the skin and the health. The water is a milky blue color and the temperature is around 36°C (97°F). You can also enjoy the views of Lake Myvatn and the surrounding volcanoes. You can buy your tickets at the entrance and the best time to go is in the evening to watch the sunset or the northern lights.

- Seljavallalaug Pool: This is one of the oldest and most hidden hot springs in Iceland. It is a natural pool that was built in 1923 and is fed by a hot spring. The water is not very hot, around 25°C (77°F), but it is enough to warm up after a hike. You can also enjoy the views of the mountains and the valley. You need to hike for 20 minutes to get to the pool and there are no facilities, so bring your own towel and swimsuit. You can go all year round, but be careful in winter as the trail can be slippery.

- Hrunalaug Hot Spring:

This is a small and cozy hot spring that is located near the town of Flúðir. It is a natural pool that can fit up to 10 people and is surrounded by a wooden fence and a hut. The water is around 38°C (100°F) and you can enjoy the views of the countryside and the sheep. There are no facilities, so bring your own towel and swimsuit. You can go all year round, but be respectful of the land and the locals who maintain the pool.

- Landbrotalaug Hot Spring: This is a tiny and secluded hot spring that is located near the Snaefellsnes Peninsula. It is a natural pool that can fit up to 4 people and is hidden in a field. The water is around 40°C (104°F) and you can enjoy the views of the mountains and the stars. There are no facilities, so bring your own towel and swimsuit. You can go all year round, but be careful of the road conditions and the weather.

- *Waterfalls*

- Gullfoss Waterfall:

This is one of the most famous and spectacular waterfalls in Iceland. It is part of the Golden Circle route and is located on the Hvítá river. It consists of two tiers that drop 32 meters (105 feet) and 21 meters (69 feet) into a canyon. You can see the waterfall from different viewpoints and feel the spray and the power of the water. You can go all year round, but be prepared for cold and windy weather.

- Skógafoss Waterfall: This is one of the most beautiful and photogenic waterfalls in Iceland. It is located on the Skógá river and is 60 meters (197 feet) high and 25 meters (82 feet) wide. You can see the waterfall from the bottom and feel the mist and the rainbow, or you can climb up to the top and see the view of the coast and the mountains. You can also hike along the river and see more waterfalls and scenery. You can go all year round, but be careful of the slippery steps and the ice in winter.

- Seljalandsfoss Waterfall:

This is one of the most unique and fun waterfalls in
Iceland. It is located on the Seljalandsá river and is
60 meters (197 feet) high. You can see the waterfall
from the front and admire its elegance and grace, or
you can walk behind it and see the view of the valley
and the sun. You can also visit the nearby Gljúfrabúi
waterfall, which is hidden in a cave. You can go all
year round, but be careful of the wet and slippery
rocks and the ice in winter.

- Dettifoss Waterfall: This is one of the most
powerful and impressive waterfalls in Iceland. It is
located on the Jökulsá á Fjöllum river and is 100
meters (328 feet) wide and 45 meters (148 feet)
high. You can see the waterfall from both sides of

the river and feel the roar and the vibration of the water. You can also visit the nearby Selfoss and Hafragilsfoss waterfalls, which are smaller but equally stunning. You can go all year round, but be careful of the road conditions and the weather.

- Svartifoss Waterfall:

This is one of the most distinctive and artistic waterfalls in Iceland. It is located in the Skaftafell Nature Reserve and is 20 meters (66 feet) high. You can see the waterfall from a short hike and admire its black basalt columns that resemble organ pipes. You can also visit the nearby Skaftafellsjökull glacier tongue and the Svínafellsjökull glacier lagoon. You can go all year round, but be careful of the weather and the terrain.

I hope these recommendations help you to enjoy the best of Iceland's hiking trails, hot springs, and waterfalls. Have a wonderful trip! ⬤

Source:
(1) 10 Best Hot Springs Trails in Iceland | AllTrails.
https://www.alltrails.com/iceland/hot-springs.

(2) 10 Epic Day Hikes in Iceland for Your Bucket List.
https://www.earthtrekkers.com/best-day-hikes-in-iceland/.

(3) 13 of the best hikes in Iceland - Lonely Planet.
https://www.lonelyplanet.com/articles/best-hikes-in-iceland.

(4) Best Iceland Itinerary Ideas From 1 Day To 2 Weeks.
https://icelandtrippers.com/iceland-itinerary/.

Tips for exploring Iceland's unique landscapes and natural wonders.

Iceland is a country of stunning natural beauty and diversity, where you can see volcanoes, glaciers, waterfalls, geysers, hot springs, and more. If you want to explore Iceland's unique landscapes and natural wonders, here are some tips for you:

- Plan your trip according to the season and the weather. Iceland has four seasons, each with its own advantages and challenges. Summer is the peak season, with long days, mild temperatures, and green scenery. However, it is also the most crowded and expensive time to visit. Winter is the low season, with short days, cold temperatures, and snowy scenery. However, it is also the best time to see the northern lights and enjoy winter activities. Spring and autumn are the shoulder seasons, with moderate weather, fewer tourists, and lower prices. However, they are also the most unpredictable seasons, with changing weather and road conditions. You should always check the weather forecast and the road conditions before you go, and be prepared for any changes.

- Rent a car or join a tour. Iceland has a well-developed road network, especially the Ring Road, which circles the island and connects most of the major attractions. Renting a car gives you the freedom and flexibility to explore Iceland at your own pace and preference. However, you should also be aware of the driving rules, the fuel costs, and the potential hazards, such as gravel roads, sheep, and weather. Alternatively, you can join a tour, which offers convenience and safety, as well as guidance and information from a local expert. However, you should also consider the cost, the schedule, and the group size of the tour, and choose the one that suits your needs and interests.

- Respect nature and culture. Iceland is a country with a fragile and diverse ecosystem, a rich and proud history, and a vibrant and creative society. You should respect and appreciate its nature and culture, and follow the rules and regulations that are in place to protect and preserve them. You should not litter, damage, or disturb the wildlife, plants, or landscapes, and you should stay on the marked trails and roads. You should also not touch, move, or take any rocks, stones, or lava, as they are considered sacred and part of the Icelandic folklore and mythology. You should also learn about and respect the customs, traditions, and beliefs of the Icelandic people, and avoid any actions or words that may offend or insult them. You should also try to experience and enjoy some of the local cuisine, music, art, and literature, and interact with the locals in a friendly and polite manner.

- Pack smart and dress in layers. Iceland's weather is unpredictable and can change quickly, from sunny and warm to rainy and cold, or even snowy and stormy. You should pack layers of clothing that are suitable for different weather conditions and activities, such as waterproof jackets, warm sweaters, thermal underwear, hats, gloves, scarves, and boots. You should also bring a swimsuit, as Iceland has many natural hot springs and geothermal pools that you can enjoy. You may also need some special equipment or gear, such as sunglasses, sunscreen, hiking shoes, sleeping bags, or tents, depending on your itinerary and preferences.

- Have fun and be adventurous. Iceland is a wonderful destination for travelers who love nature, adventure, and culture. However, it is also a country with some unique features and challenges that you should be aware of and prepared for. You should not let the weather, the prices, or the distances discourage you from exploring and enjoying Iceland. You should also not limit yourself to the most popular and visited attractions, but also seek out the hidden gems and off-the-beaten-path locations. You should also not be afraid to try new things, such as eating fermented shark, riding an Icelandic horse, or bathing in a hot spring. You should also not forget to have fun and be adventurous, as Iceland has a lot to offer, from the famous Golden Circle, Ring Road, and Diamond Circle routes, to the hidden gems and off-the-beaten-path locations [1] [2] [3].

Source:
(1) Natural Wonders of Reykjavik: Exploring Iceland's Distinctive Landscape ....
https://travelthefarthest.com/2023/04/24/reykjavik-natural-wonders-iceland-unique-landscape/.

(2) Iceland's best natural wonders - Lonely Planet.
https://www.lonelyplanet.com/articles/best-nature-spots-iceland.

(3) The 12 Most Unique Experiences in Iceland |
Guide to Iceland.
https://guidetoiceland.is/best-of-iceland/most-uniqu
e-experiences-in-iceland.

(4) 15+ Must-See Natural Wonders of Iceland -
Mindful Travel by Sara.
https://mindfultravelbysara.com/en/natural-wonders
-of-iceland/.

5. Cuisine and Dining:

Introduction to Icelandic cuisine and traditional dishes.

Icelandic cuisine is based on the ingredients that are available in the island nation, such as fish, lamb, dairy, and potatoes. Icelandic food is influenced by the Scandinavian and Nordic traditions, but also has its own unique features and flavors. Here are some of the most common and traditional dishes that you can find in Iceland, [1] [2] [3]:

- Skyr: Skyr is a dairy product that resembles yogurt, but is actually a type of soft cheese. It is made from skimmed milk that is fermented with a special culture and strained to remove the whey. Skyr is high in protein and low in fat, and has a thick and creamy texture and a mild and slightly sour taste. Skyr is eaten as a breakfast or a snack, often with berries, granola, or honey. It is also used as an ingredient in desserts, such as skyr cake or skyr ice cream.

- Hangikjöt: Hangikjöt is smoked lamb that is traditionally eaten during Christmas. The lamb is cured with salt and sugar, and then smoked over birch wood or dried sheep dung. The smoking process gives the meat a distinctive flavor and aroma, and also preserves it for a long time. Hangikjöt is usually boiled and sliced, and served with potatoes, red cabbage, green peas, and béchamel sauce. It is also eaten cold as a sandwich filling or a snack.

- Kleinur: Kleinur are twisted doughnuts that are deep-fried and sprinkled with sugar. They are a popular pastry in Iceland, and are often eaten as a treat with coffee or hot chocolate. Kleinur are made from a yeast dough that is flavored with cardamom and lemon, and shaped into knots or diamonds. They are crispy on the outside and soft on the inside, and have a sweet and spicy taste.

- Laufabrauð: Laufabrauð is a thin and crispy flatbread that is decorated with intricate patterns. It is also known as leaf bread, as the patterns resemble leaves or snowflakes. Laufabrauð is another traditional Christmas food in Iceland, and is usually made by families or friends together. The dough is rolled out very thin, and then cut with a special knife or a cookie cutter. The patterns are made by folding and cutting the dough, or by using a special tool called a laufabrauðsjárn. The bread is then fried in hot oil and eaten with butter or hangikjöt.

- Bollur: Bollur are round buns that are filled with whipped cream and jam, and topped with chocolate or powdered sugar. They are a popular dessert or snack in Iceland, and are often eaten on Bolludagur, or Bun Day, which is the Monday before Lent. Bollur are made from a sweet yeast dough that is enriched with butter and eggs, and sometimes flavored with vanilla or cardamom. The buns are baked and then cut open and filled with whipped cream and jam, usually raspberry or rhubarb. They are also sometimes filled with marzipan or chocolate.

- Plokkfiskur: Plokkfiskur is a fish stew that is made from boiled cod or haddock, potatoes, onions, and white sauce. It is a simple and hearty dish that is often eaten as a main course with dark rye bread and butter. Plokkfiskur is a way of using up leftover fish and potatoes, and each family has its own recipe and preference. Some like to mash the ingredients together, while others like to keep them whole. Some like to add cheese, mustard, or herbs, while others like to keep it plain.

- Harðfiskur: Harðfiskur is dried fish that is eaten as a snack or a starter. It is usually made from cod, haddock, or catfish, and is dried in the open air or in a special drying house. The drying process removes the water and preserves the fish, and also enhances the flavor and texture. Harðfiskur is hard and chewy, and has a strong fishy taste and smell. It is often eaten with butter, or dipped in a sauce made from sour cream, garlic, and herbs.

- Svið: Svið is a sheep's head that is singed, boiled, and served whole. It is a traditional dish that dates back to the Viking times, when nothing was wasted and every part of the animal was eaten. Svið is considered a delicacy by some, and a challenge by others. The head is split in half, and the brain is removed. The eyes, ears, tongue, and cheek are the most prized parts, and are said to be tender and tasty. Svið is usually eaten with mashed turnips and potatoes, and sometimes with a sauce made from the cooking liquid and flour.

- Hákarl: Hákarl is a fermented shark that is considered the national dish of Iceland. It is made from the Greenland shark or other sleeper sharks, which are poisonous when fresh due to the high levels of urea and trimethylamine oxide in their flesh. To make hákarl, the shark is gutted and buried in the sand for several weeks, and then hung up to dry for several months. The fermentation process breaks down the toxins and preserves the meat, but also gives it a strong ammonia smell and a pungent and fishy taste. Hákarl is usually cut into small cubes and eaten with toothpicks, often accompanied by a shot of brennivín, a local schnapps.

- Lifrarpylsa: Lifrarpylsa is a liver sausage that is made from lamb liver, suet, oatmeal, and spices. It is a traditional dish that is usually eaten in the autumn, when the sheep are slaughtered. Lifrarpylsa is cooked in a sheep's stomach or an artificial casing, and then sliced and fried or grilled. It is eaten with potatoes, turnips, and brown sauce, or with bread and butter. It has a rich and savory taste, and a soft and crumbly texture.

- Slátur: Slátur is a blood sausage that is made from lamb blood, suet, oatmeal, and spices. It is similar to lifrarpylsa, but darker and sweeter. Slátur is also cooked in a sheep's stomach or an artificial casing, and then sliced and fried or grilled. It is eaten with potatoes, turnips, and brown sauce, or with bread and butter. It has a sweet and spicy taste, and a firm and sticky texture.

- Rúgbrauð: Rúgbrauð is a dark rye bread that is baked in a pot or a special wooden cask. It is a traditional bread that is usually eaten with butter, cheese, or smoked fish. Rúgbrauð is made from rye flour, water, sugar, salt, and yeast, and sometimes flavored with caraway seeds or molasses. It is baked slowly at a low temperature, using the geothermal heat from hot springs or the steam from boiling water. The baking process gives the bread a dense and moist texture, and a slightly sweet and sour taste.

I hope this information helps you to learn more about Icelandic cuisine and traditional dishes. If you want to try some of these dishes, you can visit some of the restaurants that specialize in Icelandic food, or you can use the web search tool to find some recipes and make them at home. Enjoy! ●.

Source:
(1) Icelandic Food & Cuisine - 15 Traditional Dishes to eat in Iceland.
https://www.swedishnomad.com/icelandic-food/.

(2) Icelandic Food: 15 Traditional Dishes to Try in Iceland. https://theplanetd.com/icelandic-food/.

(3) Iceland Food: Top 15 Traditional Dishes To Try in Iceland - Reykjavik Cars.
https://www.reykjavikcars.com/blog/cuisine/Iceland-food.

(4) Icelandic Food: 12 Traditional Dishes to Eat - Christine Abroad.
https://www.christineabroad.com/icelandic-food/.

(5) Iceland Cuisine Guide: Top Recommended Dishes in Iceland.
https://www.campervaniceland.com/blog/icelandic-culture/eat-iceland-food.

(6) en.wikipedia.org.
https://en.wikipedia.org/wiki/Icelandic_cuisine.

Restaurants and Eateries.

Iceland has a variety of local restaurants and eateries that offer delicious and authentic cuisine, from seafood and lamb to pizza and burgers. Here are some recommendations for you.[1] [2] [3]:

- Seabaron:

This is a cozy and casual restaurant near the old harbor in Reykjavik, where you can enjoy some of the best seafood in town. The specialty is the lobster soup, which is rich and creamy, and served with bread and butter. You can also try the fish skewers, which are grilled on the spot and come with different sauces. The restaurant is open every day from 11:30 am to 10 pm, and you can pay by cash or card.

- Mandi: This is a small and friendly restaurant in downtown Reykjavik, where you can enjoy some spicy and flavorful Middle Eastern food. The menu includes falafel, shawarma, hummus, salads, and wraps, as well as vegetarian and vegan options. The portions are generous and the prices are reasonable. The restaurant is open every day from 11 am to 11 pm, and you can pay by cash or card.

- Kaffi Loki:

This is a charming and cozy cafe near the Hallgrimskirkja church in Reykjavik, where you can enjoy some traditional Icelandic food and drinks. The menu includes rye bread, smoked lamb, fish stew, skyr cake, and Icelandic pancakes, as well as coffee, tea, and beer. You can also enjoy the sweeping views of the city and the church from the second floor. The cafe is open every day from 9 am to 9 pm, and you can pay by cash or card.

- Bryggjan Cafe: This is a fisherman-style cafe and restaurant in Grindavik, near the Blue Lagoon. The main attraction is the lobster soup, which is made with fresh lobster, cream, and herbs, and served with bread and butter. You can also try the fish and chips, the burgers, or the salads, as well as the homemade cakes and pies. The cafe is open every day from 11 am to 9 pm, and you can pay by cash or card.

- Sushi Social:

This is a trendy and lively restaurant in Reykjavik, where you can enjoy some fusion cuisine that combines Japanese and South American flavors. The menu includes sushi, sashimi, ceviche, tacos, and steaks, as well as cocktails and desserts. The restaurant uses fresh and local ingredients, and offers a creative and colorful presentation. The restaurant is open every day from 11:30 am to 11:30 pm, and you can pay by cash or card.

- IKEA: This is a Swedish furniture store that also serves some cheap and simple food in Gardabaer, near Reykjavik. The menu includes Swedish meatballs, chicken nuggets, salads, and desserts, as well as coffee, tea, and soft drinks. The restaurant is self-service and family-friendly, and offers a nice view of the warehouse. The restaurant is open every day from 10 am to 8 pm, except on Mondays, when it is closed. You can pay by cash or card.

I hope these recommendations help you to find some local restaurants and eateries in Iceland that suit your taste and budget. Have a great time! ●

Source:
(1) 15 Best Restaurants In Iceland You Must Try - Iceland Trippers.
https://icelandtrippers.com/restaurants-in-iceland/.

(2) Where to Eat in Reykjavik: 12 Spots for Dining on a Budget.
https://guidetoiceland.is/reykjavik-guide/top-10-best-value-places-to-eat-in-reykjavik.

(3) Best Restaurants in Iceland - Tripadvisor.
https://www.tripadvisor.com/Restaurants-g189952-Iceland.html.

(4) Reykjavik's Best Restaurants for Eating Like a Local.
https://www.jacadatravel.com/polar/iceland/travel-guides/reykjaviks-best-restaurants-eating-like-local/.

(5) The 5 Best Restaurants in Iceland - Elite Traveler.
https://elitetraveler.com/finest-dining/the-5-best-restaurants-in-iceland.

6. Cultural Experiences:

Insight into Icelandic traditions, festivals, and folklore.

Festivals
Icelandic festivals are a great way to experience the culture, history, and creativity of this Nordic island nation. There are many festivals and events to celebrate throughout the year, but here are some of the most popular ones:

- Thorrablot:

This is a midwinter feast that honors the old Norse gods and the ancestors. It is held in January or February, and involves eating traditional dishes, such as fermented shark, boiled sheep's head, and blood pudding. The food is often accompanied by brennivín, a strong Icelandic schnapps[1].

- Reykjavik Winter Lights Festival: This is a festival that brightens up the dark winter nights with light installations, art exhibitions, concerts, and cultural events. It is held in February, and showcases the beauty and diversity of Reykjavik[2].

- DesignMarch:

This is a festival that celebrates Icelandic design and innovation, featuring exhibitions, workshops, lectures, and fashion shows. It is held in March, and attracts both local and international designers and visitors [3].

- Sonar Reykjavik: This is a music festival that focuses on electronic, experimental, and avant-garde music, featuring both established and emerging artists. It is held in April, and takes place in various venues, including a former power plant and a concert hall [4].

- Viking Festival:

This is a festival that recreates the life and culture of the Vikings, with historical reenactments, crafts, games, and music. It is held in June, and takes place in Hafnarfjörður, a town that is said to be home to many hidden people[5].

- National Day: This is a festival that commemorates the independence of Iceland from Denmark in 1944, with parades, speeches, concerts, and fireworks. It is held on June 17, and is a day of patriotic pride and celebration.

- Dalvik Fiskidagurinn Mikli (The Great Fish Day):

This is a festival that celebrates the fishing industry and the seafood of Iceland, with free fish soup, music, entertainment, and a fireworks show. It is held in August, and takes place in Dalvik, a small fishing town in the north of Iceland.

- Reykjavik Fringe Festival: This is a festival that showcases the alternative and experimental side of the arts, with performances, exhibitions, and workshops in various genres and disciplines. It is held in July, and takes place in various venues around Reykjavik.

- Reykjavik Jazz Festival:

This is a festival that showcases a wide range of jazz styles, from bebop to big band, performed by both established and emerging artists, including a strong representation of Icelandic musicians. The Reykjavik Jazz Festival takes place in both large and smaller venues where jazz aficionados and more casual listeners can treat themselves to some quality tunes.

- Reykjavik Culture Night:

This is a cultural extravaganza that showcases the arts, music, literature, and history of Iceland. It is held on the third Saturday of August, and offers free admission to museums, galleries, theaters, and concerts. The night ends with a spectacular fireworks show.

These are just some of the examples of the Icelandic festivals that you can enjoy. There are many more festivals and events that are unique and interesting, and you can learn more about them by visiting some of the sources that I found, such as [The Top 20 Festivals in Iceland](^1^), [10 AMAZING Festivals in Iceland You Must Go To](^2^), [What festivals are celebrated in Iceland?](^3^), [Iceland's Most Fascinating Cultural Events](^4^), and [Iceland Holidays and Festivals](^5^). 🎉.

Source:
(1) The Top 20 Festivals in Iceland | Guide to Iceland.
https://guidetoiceland.is/best-of-iceland/the-top-10-festivals-in-iceland.

(2) 10 AMAZING Festivals in Iceland You Must Go To - The Broke Backpacker.
https://www.thebrokebackpacker.com/festivals-in-iceland/.

(3) What festivals are celebrated in Iceland? | Intrepid Travel.
https://www.intrepidtravel.com/en/iceland/what-festivals-are-celebrated-iceland.

(4) Iceland's Most Fascinating Cultural Events |
Guide to Iceland.
https://guidetoiceland.is/connect-with-travel-blogge
rs/zorica/iceland-s-most-fascinating-cultural-events.

(5) Iceland Holidays and Festivals - iExplore.
https://www.iexplore.com/articles/travel-guides%2F
europe%2Ficeland%2Ffestivals-and-events.

(6) The Top 20 Festivals in Iceland | Guide to
Iceland.
https://guidetoiceland.is/best-of-iceland/the-top-10
-festivals-in-iceland.

(7) 10 AMAZING Festivals in Iceland You Must Go
To - The Broke Backpacker.
https://www.thebrokebackpacker.com/festivals-in-ic
eland/.

(8) What festivals are celebrated in Iceland? |
Intrepid Travel.
https://www.intrepidtravel.com/en/iceland/what-fes
tivals-are-celebrated-iceland.

(9) Iceland's Most Fascinating Cultural Events |
Guide to Iceland.
https://guidetoiceland.is/connect-with-travel-blogge
rs/zorica/iceland-s-most-fascinating-cultural-events.

(10) Iceland Holidays and Festivals - iExplore.
https://www.iexplore.com/articles/travel-guides%2F
europe%2Ficeland%2Ffestivals-and-events.

(11) Getty Images.
https://www.gettyimages.com/detail/photo/reykjavik
-capital-city-of-iceland-royalty-free-image/8254284
82.

Folklore

Folklore in Iceland is a fascinating topic that
reflects the culture, history, and imagination of the
Icelandic people. Folklore is the collective term for
the stories, legends, myths, and beliefs that are
passed down from generation to generation, often
orally. Folklore can serve various purposes, such as
explaining natural phenomena, teaching moral lessons,
entertaining, or preserving historical events.

Icelandic folklore is especially rich and diverse, as it draws from various sources, such as the Norse mythology, the Celtic influence, the Christian religion, and the local environment. Some of the most common themes and characters in Icelandic folklore are:

- The hidden people (huldufólk):

These are supernatural beings that resemble humans, but live in a parallel world that is invisible to most people. They are said to inhabit rocks, hills, cliffs, and waterfalls, where they have their own farms, churches, and societies. They can sometimes interact with humans, either by helping them, harming them, or falling in love with them. They are very sensitive to human actions and attitudes, and can be offended or pleased by them. They are also very protective of their homes and lands, and will not tolerate any disturbance or damage to them.

- The elves (álfar):

These are a type of hidden people that are particularly beautiful and graceful. They are often associated with nature and magic, and can bestow gifts or curses on humans. They are also very musical and artistic, and can enchant humans with their songs and dances. They are usually friendly and benevolent, but can also be vengeful and mischievous if provoked.

- The trolls (tröll):

These are large, ugly, and hairy creatures that live in the mountains and caves. They are very strong and powerful, but also very stupid and slow. They are often hostile and dangerous to humans, as they like to eat them or kidnap them. They are also afraid of sunlight, as it can turn them into stone. There are many stories of humans outwitting or escaping from trolls, or of trolls being petrified by the dawn.

- The dwarves (dvergar):

These are small, cunning, and skilled beings that live underground. They are very good at crafting and mining, and can create marvelous objects and weapons. They are also very greedy and hoard their treasures. They can sometimes help or trade with humans, but they can also trick or harm them. They are often associated with the four cardinal directions, and with the creation of the world and the first humans.

- The ghosts (draugar): These are the spirits of the dead that can haunt the living. They are usually restless and unhappy, and can cause trouble or harm to humans. They can also possess animals or objects, or shape-shift into different forms. They are often bound to their graves or burial sites, and can be appeased or exorcised by various means.

These are just some of the examples of the folklore in Iceland. There are many more stories and creatures that are unique and interesting. You can learn more about them by reading some of the sources that I found, such as [A Complete Guide to Folklore in Iceland](^1^), [The Eerie Folktales Behind Iceland's Natural Wonders](^2^), [What should I know about Icelandic folklore and mythical creatures?](^3^), [Icelandic Folklore about the Northern Lights](^4^), and [Iceland Folklore: Exploring The Legends](^5^). 🔖

Source:
(1) A Complete Guide to Folklore in Iceland | Guide to Iceland.
https://guidetoiceland.is/history-culture/folklore-in-iceland.

(2) The Eerie Folktales Behind Iceland's Natural Wonders.
https://www.nationalgeographic.com/travel/article/folklore-myths.

(3) What should I know about Icelandic folklore and mythical creatures?.
https://www.adequatetravel.com/info/iceland/what-should-i-know-about-icelandic-folklore-and-mythical-creatures.

(4) Icelandic Folklore about the Northern Lights | Perlan.
https://perlan.is/articles/icelandic-folklore-northern-lights.

(5) Iceland Folklore: Exploring The Legends | Insight Guides.
https://www.insightguides.com/inspire-me/blog/iceland-folklore-legends-in-the-land-of-ice-and-fire.

Traditions.

Icelandic traditions are the customs and practices that reflect the culture, history, and identity of the Icelandic people. Some of the most distinctive and interesting Icelandic traditions are:

- Naming: Icelanders follow a patronymic or matronymic naming system, which means that their last names are derived from their father's or mother's first name, followed by the suffix -son (son) or -dóttir (daughter). For example, if Jón has a son named Ólafur and a daughter named Sigríður, their full names would be Ólafur Jónsson and Sigríður Jónsdóttir. This tradition dates back to the Viking Age, and is still widely used today. Icelanders also have strict rules about naming their children, and must choose from a list of approved names or seek permission from the Icelandic Naming Committee[1].

- Literature: Icelanders have a strong literary tradition that goes back to the medieval sagas, which are stories of the lives and adventures of the Norse settlers and their descendants. The sagas are considered to be among the finest works of world literature, and are a source of pride and inspiration for Icelanders. Icelanders also love to read and write, and have one of the highest literacy rates and book publishing rates in the world. They have a unique Christmas tradition called Jólabókaflóð, which means "Christmas book flood", where they exchange books and read them until midnight on Christmas Eve[2].

- Food: Icelanders have a tradition of eating some unusual and exotic dishes, especially during the midwinter feast of Þorrablót, which honors the old Norse gods and the ancestors. Some of the delicacies include fermented shark (hákarl), boiled sheep's head (svið), blood pudding (blóðmör), and sour ram's testicles (hrútspungar). These foods are often accompanied by brennivín, a strong Icelandic schnapps. Icelanders also enjoy more conventional foods, such as lamb, fish, dairy products, and skyr, a thick yogurt-like product[3].

- Music: Icelanders have a vibrant and diverse music scene, ranging from folk to pop to rock to classical. Some of the most famous Icelandic musicians include Björk, Sigur Rós, Of Monsters and Men, and Kaleo. Icelanders also have a tradition of singing and composing rímur, which are epic poems that are recited or sung to a melody. Rímur are based on the sagas, the Eddas, or other historical or mythical sources, and can be very long and complex[4].

- Holidays: Icelanders celebrate various holidays throughout the year, some of which are unique to their country. Some of the most popular holidays are:
   - New Year's Eve: Icelanders celebrate the new year with bonfires, fireworks, and parties. They also have a tradition of watching a comedy show called Áramótaskaupið, which satirizes the events of the past year[5].

   - Þrettándinn:

This is the last day of Christmas, on January 6th, when the 13 Yule Lads, who are mischievous trolls that visit children during the Christmas season, return to their mountain home. Icelanders mark the occasion with bonfires, fireworks, and singing. They also believe that this is the night when the hidden people, such as elves and fairies, are most active and visible, and may offer them gifts or food.

- Sumardagurinn fyrsti: This is the first day of summer, which falls on the first Thursday after April 18th. Icelanders celebrate the arrival of warmer and brighter days with parades, sports, and entertainment. Children also receive a summer gift, usually a book or a toy.

- Sjómannadagurinn:

This is the day of the seamen, which falls on the
first Sunday of June. Icelanders honor the
fishermen and the maritime industry, which are vital
to the economy and the history of the country. They
also enjoy various activities, such as sailing, fishing,
and swimming.

- Verslunarmannahelgi: This is the merchants'
weekend, which falls on the first weekend of August.
It is the peak of the summer holiday season, and
many Icelanders travel to the countryside or attend
outdoor festivals, such as Þjóðhátíð in
Vestmannaeyjar, where they camp, sing, and watch
fireworks.

- Menningarnótt:

This is the culture night, which falls on the third Saturday of August. It is a day and night of celebrating the arts, music, literature, and history of Iceland. Museums, galleries, theaters, and concerts offer free admission, and the streets of Reykjavik are filled with people and performances. The night ends with a spectacular fireworks show.

These are some of the examples of the Icelandic traditions that you can learn about and experience. There are many more traditions that are unique and interesting, and you can find out more about them by visiting some of the sources that I found, such as [Iceland Cultures, People and Traditions Guide](^1^),

[9 Unique Icelandic Traditions You Need to Experience](^2^), [Your Guide to Iceland's Culture and Traditions](^5^), and [9 Intriguing Icelandic Traditions](^4^). 🏴

Source:
(1) Iceland Cultures, People and Traditions Guide - Iceland.org. https://www.iceland.org/culture/.

(2) 9 Unique Icelandic Traditions You Need to Experience. https://explorerchick.com/journal/unique-icelandic-traditions/.

(3) 100 Fun Facts About Iceland, Icelanders, and Icelandic Culture. https://www.heyiceland.is/blog/nanar/7337/100-fun-facts-about-iceland-icelanders-and-icelandic-culture.

(4) 9 Intriguing Icelandic Traditions — Acanela Expeditions. https://www.acanela.com/blog/9-intriguing-icelandic-traditions.

(5) Your Guide to Iceland's Culture and Traditions. https://www.discover-the-world.com/destinations/iceland-holidays/your-guide-to-icelands-culture-and-traditions/.

(6) Iceland Cultures, People and Traditions Guide - Iceland.org. https://www.iceland.org/culture/.

(7) 9 Unique Icelandic Traditions You Need to Experience. https://explorerchick.com/journal/unique-icelandic-traditions/.

(8) Your Guide to Iceland's Culture and Traditions. https://www.discover-the-world.com/destinations/iceland-holidays/your-guide-to-icelands-culture-and-traditions/.

(9) 9 Intriguing Icelandic Traditions — Acanela Expeditions. https://www.acanela.com/blog/9-intriguing-icelandic-traditions.

Suggestions for connecting with local culture and communities.

Iceland is a country with a rich and diverse culture, influenced by its history, geography, and environment. If you want to connect with the local culture and communities in Iceland, here are some suggestions:

- Take a food tour: One of the best ways to learn about a culture is through its cuisine. Iceland has a variety of dishes that reflect its natural resources, such as seafood, lamb, dairy, and berries. You can join a food tour that will take you to different restaurants and cafes, where you can sample traditional and modern Icelandic delicacies, such as skyr, hákarl, rúgbrauð, and kleinur. A food tour will also give you a chance to interact with local chefs and foodies, and learn about the history and stories behind each dish[1].

- Join a knitting class: Knitting is a popular hobby and craft in Iceland, and many people wear hand-knitted sweaters, hats, and scarves made from Icelandic wool. Knitting is also a way of expressing creativity and identity, as well as preserving a cultural heritage. You can join a knitting class that will teach you the basics of knitting, as well as the patterns and techniques that are unique to Icelandic knitting. You can also buy some yarn and needles from a local shop, and make your own souvenir or gift[1].

- Visit Hallgrimskirkja Church:

Hallgrimskirkja is the most iconic landmark in Reykjavik, and one of the tallest buildings in Iceland. It is a Lutheran church that was designed by the architect Guðjón Samúelsson, who was inspired by the basalt columns and glaciers of Iceland. The church has a striking appearance, with a tower that resembles a rocket, and a facade that resembles an organ. The church also has a large pipe organ, and hosts regular concerts and events. You can visit the church and admire its architecture, as well as climb up the tower and enjoy a panoramic view of the city [1].

- Explore the Wonders of Iceland exhibition: If you want to learn more about the natural phenomena and wonders of Iceland, such as volcanoes, glaciers, geysers, and northern lights, you can visit the Wonders of Iceland exhibition in Perlan. Perlan is a museum and observation deck that is located on a hill in Reykjavik, and offers a 360-degree view of the surroundings. The Wonders of Iceland exhibition features interactive displays, simulations, and models that explain the science and beauty of Iceland's nature. You can also experience a real ice cave, and see a replica of a geyser erupt [4].

- Participate in a cultural and heritage course: If you want to have a deeper and more comprehensive understanding of the culture and heritage of Iceland, you can participate in a course that will cover various aspects of Icelandic society, such as history, literature, art, music, and sustainability. You can choose a course that suits your interests and needs, and learn from experts and locals who will share their knowledge and insights. You can also visit different sites and locations that are relevant to the course, such as museums, galleries, monuments, and natural attractions. A cultural and heritage course will also give you an opportunity to network and collaborate with other participants, and create your own culture and heritage project[2].

Source:
(1) Iceland Cultures, People and Traditions Guide - Iceland.org. https://www.iceland.org/culture/.

(2) Creating Connection Between Communities - Iceland Monitor. https://icelandmonitor.mbl.is/news/culture_and_livin g/2021/06/21/creating_connection_between_commu nities/.

(3) CULTURE AND HERITAGE IN ICELAND. A SUSTAINABLE LIFESTYLE CONNECTED WITH .... https://school-education.ec.europa.eu/en/profession al-development/courses/culture-and-heritage-iceland -sustainable-lifestyle-connected-local.

(4) The Best Cultural Activities To Take Part in While in Iceland - Matador ....
https://matadornetwork.com/read/food-tours-knitting-classes-volcano-hikes-best-ways-learn-icelandic-culture-way-life/.

(5) Local Culture in Iceland - Wonderguide.
https://wonderguide.com/iceland/explore/local-culture-iceland.

7. Practical Tips:

Transportation options within Iceland.

Transportation options within Iceland are varied and depend on your budget, preferences, and itinerary. Here are some of the main ways to get around the country:

- Car rental: This is the most popular and flexible option for many travelers, as it allows you to explore the country at your own pace and visit remote and scenic locations. You can rent a car at the airport or in Reykjavik, and choose from different types and sizes of vehicles, depending on the season and the roads you plan to drive on. You can also book a self-drive tour package, which includes accommodation, itinerary, and activities. Driving in Iceland requires some caution and preparation, as the weather and road conditions can change quickly and dramatically. You should always check the weather and road reports before you set off, and follow the speed limits and traffic rules. You should also be aware of some specific hazards, such as sheep, blind hills, narrow bridges, and gravel roads[1].

- Bus: This is a cheaper and more eco-friendly option than car rental, but also less convenient and flexible. There are several bus companies that operate routes around the Ring Road, the Westfjords, and the Highlands (in summer only). You can buy single tickets, day passes, or multi-day passes, depending on your travel plans. Buses are generally comfortable and reliable, but they run on fixed schedules and may not stop at all the places you want to see. You may also need to book your tickets in advance, especially during peak season[2].

- Plane: This is the fastest and most comfortable option for traveling long distances within Iceland, but also the most expensive and least scenic. There are domestic flights from Reykjavik to Akureyri, Egilsstaðir, Ísafjörður, and the Westman Islands, operated by Icelandair and Air Iceland Connect. Flights are usually short and frequent, but they can be affected by weather conditions and cancellations. You may also need to pay extra for luggage and transfers. Flying within Iceland can save you time and allow you to visit remote regions, but you will miss out on the stunning landscapes and attractions along the way[3].

- Taxi: This is a convenient and comfortable option for short trips within Reykjavik or other towns, but also very expensive and not very eco-friendly. You can find taxis at the airport, hotels, or taxi stands, or call them by phone or app. Taxis are metered and charge a base fare plus a per-kilometer rate. You can pay by cash or card, and tips are not expected. Taxis are not a practical option for traveling around the country, as they can cost a fortune and may not be available in rural areas[4].

- Hitchhiking: This is a cheap and adventurous option for traveling around Iceland, but also risky and unreliable. Hitchhiking is legal and relatively safe in Iceland, as most people are friendly and helpful. However, it is not very common and not recommended, especially for solo travelers, women, or in winter. You may have to wait a long time for a ride, or not get one at all. You may also encounter some dangers or difficulties, such as bad weather, language barriers, or dishonest drivers. If you decide to hitchhike, you should always use common sense and caution, and follow some basic rules, such as carrying a sign, choosing a good spot, dressing appropriately, and trusting your instincts[5].

These are some of the main transportation options within Iceland. You can also travel by boat, bike, helicopter, or guided tour, depending on your interests and budget. You can find more information and tips on how to get around Iceland by visiting some of the sources that I found, such as [How To Get Around Iceland - 10 Transportation Options](^1^), [The Ultimate Guide to Transport in Iceland](^2^), [How to get around in Iceland with public transportation](^3^), [Is there Uber in Iceland? 17 Great Alternative Travel Options](^4^), and [Public transport in Iceland](^5^). 🚗🚌✈️🛥️👍

Source:
(1) How To Get Around Iceland - 10 Transportation Options - Iceland with a View. https://icelandwithaview.com/iceland-transportation-options/.

(2) The Ultimate Guide to Transport in Iceland | Guide to Iceland.

https://guidetoiceland.is/travel-info/the-ultimate-gu
ide-to-transport-in-iceland.

(3) How to get around in Iceland with public
transportation.
https://www.funiceland.is/facts/travel-guide/public-
transportation/.

(4) Is there Uber in Iceland? 17 Great Alternative
Travel Options.
https://coupletraveltheworld.com/uber-in-iceland/.

(5) Public transport in Iceland.
https://www.visiticeland.com/article/public-transpor
t/.

(6) How To Get Around Iceland - 10 Transportation
Options - Iceland with a View.
https://icelandwithaview.com/iceland-transportation
-options/.

(7) The Ultimate Guide to Transport in Iceland |
Guide to Iceland.
https://guidetoiceland.is/travel-info/the-ultimate-gu
ide-to-transport-in-iceland.

(8) How to get around in Iceland with public transportation.
https://www.funiceland.is/facts/travel-guide/public-transportation/.

(9) Is there Uber in Iceland? 17 Great Alternative Travel Options.
https://coupletraveltheworld.com/uber-in-iceland/.

(10) Public transport in Iceland.
https://www.visiticeland.com/article/public-transport/.

Accommodation recommendations for different budgets.

Iceland is a beautiful and diverse country that attracts many visitors every year. However, it is also known to be quite expensive, especially when it comes to accommodation. Therefore, it is important to plan ahead and find the best options for your budget and preferences. Here are some accommodation recommendations for different budgets in Iceland:

- Budget: If you are looking for the cheapest way to stay in Iceland, camping is your best option. Camping is very popular and widely available in Iceland, and you can find many campgrounds around the country, especially along the Ring Road. Camping fees range from 1,500 to 2,300 ISK per person ($11 to $18) per night, and some campgrounds offer facilities such as showers, toilets, electricity, and wifi. You can bring your own tent and equipment, or rent them from various companies in Reykjavik or at the airport [1]. Another budget option is staying in hostels, which are also common and affordable in Iceland. Hostels offer dorm beds or private rooms with shared bathrooms, and usually have communal kitchens, lounges, and laundry facilities. Hostels charge around $30 per dorm bed or $120 per private room per night, and you can book them online or on arrival [2].

- Mid-range: If you have a moderate budget and want more comfort and privacy, you can opt for guesthouses, bed and breakfasts, or cottages. These are cozy and charming accommodations that offer private rooms or apartments with ensuite bathrooms, and sometimes include breakfast or kitchen facilities. They are usually family-run and located in scenic or rural areas, giving you a chance to experience the local culture and nature. They charge around $150 to $275 per night, depending on the season and location, and you can book them online or by phone [3]. Another mid-range option is staying in apartments, which are spacious and modern accommodations that offer fully-equipped kitchens, living rooms, and bedrooms. They are ideal for families or groups of friends who want more space and flexibility. They are mostly located in Reykjavik or other towns, giving you easy access to shops, restaurants, and attractions. They charge around $200 to $300 per night, and you can book them online through platforms such as Airbnb or Booking.com [4].

- Luxury: If you have a high budget and want to splurge on your accommodation, you can choose from a variety of hotels, apartment hotels, or igloo hotels. Hotels are the most common and luxurious accommodations in Iceland, offering private rooms or suites with ensuite bathrooms, and amenities such as restaurants, bars, spas, and pools. They are usually located in Reykjavik or other major towns, or near popular attractions such as the Blue Lagoon or the

Golden Circle. They charge around $300 to $500 per night, and you can book them online or by phone[5]. Apartment hotels are similar to hotels, but offer larger and more stylish apartments with kitchens, living rooms, and bedrooms. They are perfect for travelers who want the best of both worlds: the comfort and service of a hotel, and the space and privacy of an apartment. They are mostly located in Reykjavik, and charge around $400 to $600 per night. Igloo hotels are a unique and adventurous option for staying in Iceland, especially in winter. They are transparent domes that offer panoramic views of the sky and the landscape, and are equipped with cozy beds, heaters, and lights. They are ideal for couples or solo travelers who want to experience the northern lights or the midnight sun from their bed. They are located in remote and scenic areas, such as the Thingvellir National Park or the Seljalandsfoss waterfall, and charge around $500 to $700 per night.

I hope this gives you some ideas on where to stay in Iceland for different budgets. You can find more information and tips on accommodation in Iceland by visiting some of the sources that I found, such as

[Where to stay in Iceland - COMPLETE Guide to Accommodation](^1^), [Accommodations in Iceland](^2^), [Iceland Trip Cost + 39 Sneaky Budget Tips](^3^), [The Best Accommodation in Iceland](^4^), and [12 Best Akureyri Hotels And Hostels For All Budgets](^5^). 🌋🏠⬛

Source:
(1) Where to stay in Iceland - COMPLETE Guide to Accommodation - Miss Tourist. https://misstourist.com/icelands-best-hotels-an-easy-way-to-book-accommodation-before-your-trip/.

(2) Accommodations in Iceland. https://www.visiticeland.com/accommodations/.

(3) Iceland Trip Cost + 39 Sneaky Budget Tips | Two Wandering Soles. https://www.twowanderingsoles.com/blog/travel-budget-for-one-week-in-iceland.

(4) The Best Accommodation in Iceland | Guide to Iceland. https://guidetoiceland.is/accommodation.

(5) 12 Best Akureyri Hotels And Hostels For All Budgets - Iceland Trippers. https://icelandtrippers.com/akureyri-hotels/.

(6) Where to stay in Iceland - COMPLETE Guide to Accommodation - Miss Tourist. https://misstourist.com/icelands-best-hotels-an-easy-way-to-book-accommodation-before-your-trip/.

(7) Accommodations in Iceland. https://www.visiticeland.com/accommodations/.

(8) Iceland Trip Cost + 39 Sneaky Budget Tips | Two Wandering Soles. https://www.twowanderingsoles.com/blog/travel-budget-for-one-week-in-iceland.

(9) The Best Accommodation in Iceland | Guide to Iceland. https://guidetoiceland.is/accommodation.

(10) 12 Best Akureyri Hotels And Hostels For All Budgets - Iceland Trippers. https://icelandtrippers.com/akureyri-hotels/.

Safety guidelines and emergency information.

Iceland is a safe and peaceful country, but it also has some natural hazards and challenges that you should be aware of and prepared for. Here are some safety guidelines and emergency information for traveling in Iceland:

- Weather and road conditions: Iceland's weather is unpredictable and can change rapidly, especially in winter. You should always check the weather forecast and the road conditions before you travel, and adjust your plans accordingly. You can use the SafeTravel Iceland App or visit [safetravel.is](^1^) for the latest updates and alerts. You should also dress appropriately for the weather, and bring warm and waterproof clothing, shoes, and accessories. If you are driving, you should follow the speed limits and traffic rules, and be careful of slippery roads, blind hills, narrow bridges, and gravel roads. You should also avoid driving in the dark, in bad weather, or on closed roads. You can find more tips on driving in Iceland [here](^2^).

- Natural hazards: Iceland is a volcanic and geothermal country, which means that it has some natural phenomena that can pose a risk to travelers, such as earthquakes, volcanic eruptions, avalanches, landslides, and geysers. You should always respect the nature and follow the signs and instructions that are given to you by the authorities or the guides. You should also stay on marked paths and trails, and avoid walking on unstable or hot ground, near cliffs or waterfalls, or in restricted areas. You can learn more about the natural hazards in Iceland [here](^3^).

- Emergency services: In case of an emergency, you should always call 112, which is the national emergency number in Iceland. You can also use the 112 Iceland App, which allows you to send your location to the emergency services. The emergency services in Iceland include the police, the ambulance, the fire brigade, and the ICE-SAR (Icelandic Association for Search and Rescue), which is a volunteer-based organization that specializes in providing search and rescue services in remote and difficult areas. You can find more information about the emergency services in Iceland [here](^4^).

- Health care: Iceland has a high-quality and universal health care system, which means that everyone has access to medical services and treatments. However, as a foreign traveler, you may have to pay for some or all of the costs, depending on your insurance and the type of service. You should always have a valid travel insurance that covers your medical expenses and repatriation in case of an emergency. You should also bring your European Health Insurance Card (EHIC) if you are a citizen of the European Union or the European Economic Area, as it can reduce or waive some of the fees. You can find more information about the healthcare system in Iceland [here].

I hope this gives you some useful information on how to stay safe and healthy in Iceland. Iceland is a wonderful country to visit, but it also requires some caution and preparation. You can find more resources and tips on safety and emergency in Iceland by visiting [safetravel.is](^1^), which is the official source for safe travel in Iceland. 🏴.

Source: (1) Safetravel - Be safe in Iceland. https://safetravel.is/.

(2) Safetravel - Everything you need to know for a safe trip to Iceland.
https://www.visiticeland.com/article/safe-travel-in-iceland/.

(3) Travel advice and advisories for Iceland.
https://travel.gc.ca/destinations/iceland.

(4) Iceland Travel Advisory.
https://travel.state.gov/content/travel/en/traveladvisories/traveladvisories/iceland-travel-advisory.html.

(5) Safetravel - Be safe in Iceland.
https://safetravel.is/.

(6) Getty Images.
https://www.gettyimages.com/detail/photo/reykjavik-capital-city-of-iceland-royalty-free-image/825428482.

8. Activities and Excursions:

Suggestions for tours, excursions, and activities such as Northern Lights tours or whale watching.

Iceland is a country that offers a wide range of tours, excursions, and activities for travelers of all interests and preferences. Whether you want to explore the natural wonders, experience the culture and history, or enjoy some adventure and fun, you will find something to suit your taste in Iceland. Here are some suggestions for tours, excursions, and activities in Iceland, based on different categories:

- Nature and scenery: Iceland is famous for its stunning and diverse landscapes, such as glaciers, volcanoes, waterfalls, geysers, and hot springs. You can admire these natural attractions by joining various tours, such as the Golden Circle tour, which covers the most iconic sights of Iceland, such as Thingvellir National Park, Geysir geothermal area, and Gullfoss waterfall[1]. You can also visit the South Coast, which boasts some of the most beautiful scenery in the country, such as Seljalandsfoss and Skogafoss waterfalls, Reynisfjara black sand beach, and Jokulsarlon glacier lagoon[2]. If you want to see more of the country, you can take a tour of the Ring Road, which circles the island and passes through many regions and attractions, such as the Snaefellsnes peninsula, the Westfjords, the Eastfjords, and the Lake Myvatn area[3].

- Culture and history: Iceland has a rich and fascinating culture and history, dating back to the Viking Age and the medieval sagas. You can learn more about the country's heritage and traditions by visiting various museums, galleries, and cultural sites, such as the National Museum of Iceland

, the Reykjavik Art Museum

, and

the Saga Museum[4]

.You

can also explore some of the historical and archaeological sites, such as Thingvellir, where the first parliament was established in 930 AD, Reykholt, where the famous saga writer Snorri Sturluson lived, and Skalholt, where the first bishopric was founded in 1056 AD[5]. If you want to experience the local culture and lifestyle, you can also join some of the festivals and events that are held throughout the year, such as the Reykjavik Culture Night

the Thorrablot midwinter feast

, and
the Gay Pride parade[6]

.

- Adventure and fun: Iceland is a paradise for
adventure and fun seekers, as it offers many

activities and sports that will get your adrenaline pumping and your spirits soaring. You can try some of the winter activities, such as skiing, snowboarding, snowmobiling, and ice skating, or some of the summer activities, such as hiking, biking, kayaking, and rafting. You can also experience some of the unique and thrilling activities that Iceland has to offer, such as snorkeling or diving in the Silfra fissure, which is a crack between the North American and Eurasian tectonic plates, or going inside a volcano, which is a dormant magma chamber that you can descend into by a cable lift. If you want to have some fun and relaxation, you can also visit some of the geothermal pools and spas, such as the Blue Lagoon, which is a mineral-rich lagoon that has healing and rejuvenating properties, or the Secret Lagoon, which is a natural hot spring that has a rustic and authentic charm.

These are some of the suggestions for tours, excursions, and activities in Iceland. You can find more information and options by visiting some of the sources that I found, such as [The Top 10 Best Tours in Iceland: Popular and Unique Excursions](^2^), [Plan and book Iceland tours and activities](^4^), [25 Best

Things to Do in Iceland](^5^), and [THE 10 BEST
Iceland Tours & Excursions for 2023](^6^). 🏴

Source:
 (1) THE 10 BEST Iceland Tours & Excursions for
2023 (with Prices) - Tripadvisor.
https://www.tripadvisor.com/Attractions-g189952-A
ctivities-c42-Iceland.html.

(2) The Top 10 Best Tours in Iceland: Popular and
Unique Excursions.
https://guidetoiceland.is/best-of-iceland/top-10-tou
rs-in-iceland.

(3) Top Activities in Iceland for Adrenaline Junkies -
Guide to Iceland.
https://guidetoiceland.is/best-of-iceland/the-most-t
hrilling-activities-in-iceland.

(4) Plan and book Iceland tours and activities - Stuck
in Iceland Travel ....
https://www.stuckiniceland.com/iceland-tours-and-ac
tivities/.

(5) 25 Best Things to Do in Iceland - Travel + Leisure.
https://www.travelandleisure.com/best-things-to-do-in-iceland-7965359.

(6) THE 10 BEST Iceland Tours & Excursions for 2023 (with Prices) - Tripadvisor.
https://www.tripadvisor.ca/Attractions-g189952-Activities-c42-Iceland.html.

(7) The Top 10 Best Tours in Iceland: Popular and Unique Excursions.
https://guidetoiceland.is/best-of-iceland/top-10-tours-in-iceland.

(8) Plan and book Iceland tours and activities - Stuck in Iceland Travel ....
https://www.stuckiniceland.com/iceland-tours-and-activities/.

(9) 25 Best Things to Do in Iceland - Travel + Leisure.
https://www.travelandleisure.com/best-things-to-do-in-iceland-7965359.

(10) THE 10 BEST Iceland Tours & Excursions for 2023 (with Prices) - Tripadvisor. https://www.tripadvisor.ca/Attractions-g189952-Activities-c42-Iceland.html.

Outdoor and adventure activities suitable for various interests.

Iceland is a paradise for outdoor and adventure lovers, as it offers a variety of activities that suit different interests and levels of difficulty. Whether you want to enjoy the stunning scenery, experience the thrill of nature, or challenge yourself physically, you will find something to satisfy your curiosity and passion in Iceland. Here are some examples of outdoor and adventure activities that you can try in Iceland, based on different categories:

- Water activities: Iceland is surrounded by water, and has many rivers, lakes, and geothermal pools that invite you to explore and enjoy them. You can try snorkeling or diving in the Silfra fissure, which is a crack between the North American and Eurasian tectonic plates, and marvel at the crystal-clear water and the underwater scenery[1]. You can also go whale watching in Dalvik, and see some of the majestic marine mammals that inhabit the Icelandic waters, such as humpback whales, minke whales, and dolphins[2]. If you are looking for some excitement, you can go white water rafting in the Hvita river, and experience the rapids, waves, and drops that will make your heart race[3].

- Ice activities: Iceland is also known as the land of ice and fire, and has many glaciers and ice caves that offer a unique and adventurous experience. You can go glacier hiking on the Sólheimajökull or Vatnajökull glaciers, and walk on the ancient ice, see the crevasses, moulins, and ice sculptures, and learn about the glacier's formation and movement[4]. You can also go ice caving in the Vatnajökull glacier, and enter the magical world of blue ice, where you can see the different shapes, textures, and colors of the ice[5]. If you want to have some fun and speed, you can go snowmobiling on the Langjökull glacier, and enjoy the panoramic views of the snowy landscape.

- Land activities: Iceland has a diverse and beautiful terrain, and has many trails, mountains, and volcanoes that are perfect for hiking, biking, and riding. You can go hiking in the central highlands, such as Landmannalaugar or Thorsmork, and see the colorful rhyolite mountains, the geothermal springs, and the lush valleys. You can also go biking in the Snaefellsnes peninsula, and cycle along the coast, the lava fields, and the glacier. If you want to experience the Icelandic culture and nature, you can go horseback riding, and ride the friendly and sturdy Icelandic horses, which have a unique gait called tölt, through the countryside, the beaches, or the mountains.

These are just some of the examples of outdoor and adventure activities that you can do in Iceland. There are many more options and possibilities that you can find by visiting some of the sources that I found, such as [Popular Activities in Iceland](^1^), [The Top 9 Adventures in Iceland](^2^), [The Best Winter Activities in Iceland](^3^), and [Popular Activities in Iceland](^4^). ■

Source:
 (1) The Top 9 Adventures in Iceland | Guide to Iceland.
https://guidetoiceland.is/best-of-iceland/top-9-adventures-in-iceland.

(2) THE 10 BEST Outdoor Activities in Iceland (Updated 2023) - Tripadvisor. https://www.tripadvisor.com/Attractions-g189952-Activities-c61-Iceland.html.

(3) Popular Activities in Iceland | Arctic Adventures. https://adventures.is/iceland/day-tours/popular-activities/.

(4) The Best Winter Activities in Iceland | Guide to Iceland. https://guidetoiceland.is/best-of-iceland/best-winter-activities-in-iceland.

(5) Popular Activities in Iceland | Adventures.com. https://adventures.com/iceland/tours/activities/.

(6) The Top 9 Adventures in Iceland | Guide to Iceland. https://guidetoiceland.is/best-of-iceland/top-9-adventures-in-iceland.

(7) THE 10 BEST Outdoor Activities in Iceland (Updated 2023) - Tripadvisor.

https://www.tripadvisor.com/Attractions-g189952-A
ctivities-c61-Iceland.html.

(8) Popular Activities in Iceland | Arctic Adventures.
https://adventures.is/iceland/day-tours/popular-acti
vities/.

(9) The Best Winter Activities in Iceland | Guide to
Iceland.
https://guidetoiceland.is/best-of-iceland/best-winte
r-activities-in-iceland.

9. Packing Guide:

Things to pack.

Iceland is a beautiful country with diverse landscapes and weather conditions. Depending on the season, you may need different items to pack for your trip. Here is a general guide on what to bring and what not to bring for each season:

Winter (December to February)
- Winter in Iceland can be very cold, windy, and snowy. The average temperature is around 0°C (32°F), but it can drop below -10°C (14°F) at night. The daylight hours are also very short, with only about 4 to 5 hours of sunlight per day.
- To stay warm and comfortable, you should pack the following items:
   - A warm and waterproof parka or coat, preferably with a hood. You can also layer a fleece jacket or sweater underneath for extra warmth. [This parka] for women and [this one] for men are good options.
   - Waterproof and insulated boots with good traction, such as [these hiking boots] for women and [these ones] for men. You may also want to bring

crampons or spikes to attach to your boots for walking on icy surfaces.

- Thermal underwear, such as [this set] for women and [this set] for men. These will help you retain body heat and wick away moisture.

- Fleece-lined leggings or pants, such as [these leggings] for women and [these pants] for men. You can wear them over your thermal underwear or under your rain pants for extra insulation.

- Rain pants, such as [these ones] for women and [these ones] for men. These will protect you from the wind and the snow, and keep you dry.

- Wool or synthetic socks, such as [these socks] for women and [these socks] for men. You should bring several pairs and change them often to avoid getting blisters or frostbite.

- A wool or fleece hat, scarf, and gloves, such as [this hat], [this scarf], and [these gloves] for women and [this hat], [this scarf], and [these gloves] for men. These will cover your head, neck, and hands from the cold and the wind.

- A swimsuit and a quick-dry towel, such as [this bikini] for women and [these trunks] for men and [this towel]. You may want to visit one of the many hot springs or geothermal pools in Iceland, such as the famous Blue Lagoon. A towel is not always provided, so it's better to bring your own.

- A flashlight or a headlamp, such as [this one]. Since the days are very short, you may need some extra light for your outdoor activities or for spotting the northern lights.

- A power adapter, such as [this one]. Iceland uses the European-style plug with two round prongs and 220 volts/50Hz. You may need an adapter to charge your devices or use your appliances.

- A windproof travel umbrella, such as [this one]. Iceland is very rainy, especially in the south and west parts of the country. An umbrella will help you stay dry and shield you from the wind.

- A camera and a tripod, such as [this camera] and [this tripod]. Iceland is a photographer's paradise, with stunning scenery and natural phenomena. A tripod will help you capture the northern lights, the waterfalls, the glaciers, and other amazing sights.
- You should NOT bring the following items:

- High heels or dress shoes. These are not practical or comfortable for walking on the uneven or slippery terrain. You may also damage them with the salt or the mud.

- Cotton clothing. Cotton absorbs moisture and takes a long time to dry, which can make you feel cold and uncomfortable. You should opt for wool or synthetic fabrics instead, which are more breathable and quick-drying.
- Heavy or bulky luggage. You may have to carry your luggage over long distances or up and down stairs, especially if you are staying in guesthouses or hostels. You should pack light and use a backpack or a duffel bag instead of a suitcase.

Spring (March to May)
- Spring in Iceland is a transitional season, with unpredictable weather and changing conditions. The average temperature is around 3°C (37°F), but it can vary from -5°C (23°F) to 10°C (50°F). The daylight hours are also increasing, with about 10 to 16 hours of sunlight per day.
- To be prepared for any situation, you should pack the following items:
  - A waterproof and windproof jacket or coat, such as [this jacket] for women and [this jacket] for men. You can also layer a fleece jacket or sweater underneath for extra warmth. [This fleece jacket]

for women and [this fleece jacket] for men are good
options.

- Waterproof and sturdy shoes with good traction,
such as [these hiking shoes] for women and [these
hiking shoes] for men. You may also want to bring
crampons or spikes to attach to your shoes for
walking on icy surfaces.

- Thermal underwear, such as [this set] for women
and [this set] for men. These will help you retain
body heat and wick away moisture.

- Fleece-lined leggings or pants, such as [these
leggings] for women and [these pants] for men. You
can wear them over your thermal underwear or under
your rain pants for extra insulation.

- Rain pants, such as [these ones] for women and
[these ones] for men. These will protect you from
the wind and the rain, and keep you dry.

- Wool or synthetic socks, such as [these socks]
for women and [these socks] for men. You should
bring several pairs and change them often to avoid
getting blisters or frostbite.

- A wool or fleece hat, scarf, and gloves, such as
[this hat], [this scarf], and [these gloves] for women
and [this hat], [this scarf], and [these gloves] for

men. These will cover your head, neck, and hands from the cold and the wind.

- A swimsuit and a quick-dry towel, such as [this bikini] for women and [these trunks] for men and [this towel]. You may want to visit one of the many hot springs or geothermal pools in Iceland, such as the famous Blue Lagoon. A towel is not always provided, so it's better to bring your own.

- A power adapter, such as [this one]. Iceland uses the European-style plug with two round prongs and 220 volts/50Hz. You may need an adapter to charge your devices or use your appliances.

- A windproof travel umbrella, such as [this one]. Iceland is very rainy, especially in the south and west parts of the country. An umbrella will help you stay dry and shield you from the wind.

- A camera and a tripod, such as [this camera] and [this tripod]. Iceland is a photographer's paradise, with stunning scenery and natural phenomena. A tripod will help you capture the northern lights, the waterfalls, the glaciers, and other amazing sights.
- You should NOT bring the following items:

- High heels or dress shoes. These are not practical or comfortable for walking on the uneven or slippery terrain. You may also damage them with the salt or the mud.

   - Cotton clothing. Cotton absorbs moisture and takes a long time to dry, which can make you feel cold and uncomfortable. You should opt for wool or synthetic fabrics instead, which are more breathable and quick-drying.

   - Heavy or bulky luggage. You may have to carry your luggage over long distances or up and down stairs, especially if you are staying in guesthouses or hostels. You should pack light and use a backpack or a duffel bag instead of a suitcase.

Summer (June to August)
- Summer in Iceland is the warmest and brightest season, with mild weather and long days. The average temperature is around 10°C (50°F), but it can range from 5°C (41°F) to 15°C (59°F). The daylight hours are also very long, with up to 24 hours of sunlight per day during the summer solstice.

- To enjoy the summer activities and attractions, you should pack the following items:
   - A waterproof and windproof jacket or coat, such as [this jacket] for women and [this jacket] for men.

You can also layer a fleece jacket or sweater underneath for extra warmth. [This fleece jacket] for women and [this fleece jacket] for men are good options.

   - Waterproof and sturdy shoes with good traction, such as [these hiking shoes] for women and [these hiking shoes] for

Source:
 (1) What to Pack for a Trip to Iceland: A Complete Packing List - Travel.
https://www.travelandleisure.com/iceland-vacation-packing-list-6832347.

(2) 27 Top Iceland Packing List Items for 2023 - Asher & Lyric.
https://www.asherfergusson.com/must-have-iceland-packing-list-items/.

(3) Packing for Iceland: What to Bring and What NOT to Bring.
https://playiceland.is/packing-for-iceland-what-to-bring-and-what-not-to-bring/.

(4) Iceland Packing List: What to Pack for a Trip to Iceland.
https://ordinarytraveler.com/iceland-packing-guide.

(5) What to pack for Iceland : Pack for your trip : Iceland Travel Guide.
https://iceland.nordicvisitor.com/travel-guide/information/what-to-pack/.

Tips on what to wear and how to prepare for changing weather conditions.

Iceland is a country with diverse and unpredictable weather conditions, especially in winter. Therefore, it is important to be prepared for any situation and dress accordingly. Here are some tips on what to wear and how to prepare for changing weather conditions in Iceland:

- The key to dressing for Iceland is layering. You should wear multiple layers of clothing that you can easily add or remove depending on the temperature, wind, and precipitation. The basic layers are: a thermal base layer, a mid layer, and an outer layer.

You can also add accessories like a hat, scarf, gloves, and sunglasses.

- The thermal base layer is the layer that touches your skin and helps you retain body heat and wick away moisture. You should choose a material that is breathable and quick-drying, such as wool, fleece, or synthetic fabrics. Avoid cotton, as it absorbs moisture and takes a long time to dry, which can make you feel cold and uncomfortable. You should wear thermal underwear, such as leggings and a long-sleeved shirt, for both your upper and lower body.

- The mid layer is the layer that provides insulation and warmth. You should choose a material that is lightweight and cozy, such as fleece, wool, or down. You can wear a fleece-lined or wool sweater, a fleece or down jacket, or a fleece-lined or wool skirt or pants. You can also layer multiple mid layers depending on the weather and your preference.

- The outer layer is the layer that protects you from the wind and the rain. You should choose a material that is waterproof and windproof, such as Gore-Tex, nylon, or polyester. You should wear a rainproof and windproof jacket and trousers, preferably with a hood, zippers, and pockets. You can also opt for a parka or a coat if you need extra warmth and coverage.

- The accessories are the items that cover your head, neck, hands, feet, and eyes. You should choose materials that are warm and durable, such as wool, fleece, leather, or synthetic fabrics. You should wear a wool or fleece hat, scarf, and gloves, a pair of wool or synthetic socks, a pair of waterproof and sturdy shoes or boots with good traction, and a pair of sunglasses or goggles. You can also bring a buff, a balaclava, or a face mask for extra protection from the wind and the cold.

- To prepare for changing weather conditions in Iceland, you should always check the weather forecast before you go out and plan your activities accordingly. You should also pack a backpack with some essential items, such as a water bottle, a snack, a flashlight, a power adapter, a camera, a tripod, a map, a compass, a first aid kit, and a whistle. You should also bring a windproof travel umbrella, a sleep mask, a swimsuit, and a quick-dry towel, in case you want to visit a hot spring or a geothermal pool. You should also have some spare clothes and accessories in case you get wet or dirty.

You can find more information and examples from the web search results that I used to create this response[1][2][3][45]. Have a great day! ⬤.

Source:
(1) What to Wear in Iceland | Your Iceland Packing List - Arctic Adventures.
https://adventures.is/blog/the-weather-iceland-how-to-dress/.

(2) What to Wear in Iceland in Winter (October-April): Packing List & Tips.
https://fullsuitcase.com/iceland-packing-essentials-winter/.

(3) What to wear in Iceland : Nordic Visitor.
https://www.nordicvisitor.com/blog/what-to-pack-for-your-trip-to-iceland/.

(4) Tips for Iceland in Winter: Weather and Packing Guide.

https://www.icelandtours.is/blog/iceland-winter-weather-what-to-pack/.

(5) Travel to Iceland in winter: weather conditions, what to wear, how to ....

https://www.icelandair.com/blog/winter-travel-in-iceland/.

(6) Getty Images.

https://www.gettyimages.com/detail/photo/reykjavik-capital-city-of-iceland-royalty-free-image/825428482.

10. Photography and Souvenirs:

Photography tips for capturing the beauty of Iceland.

Iceland is a stunning destination for photography, with its diverse and dramatic landscapes, natural phenomena, and wildlife. However, it can also be challenging to capture its beauty, as the weather can be unpredictable, the light can be harsh, and the conditions can be harsh. Here are some photography tips for capturing the beauty of Iceland:

- Use a wide-angle lens. A wide-angle lens can help you capture the vastness and scale of Iceland's scenery, such as the waterfalls, glaciers, mountains, and volcanoes. It can also create a sense of depth and perspective, by emphasizing the foreground and minimizing the background. A wide-angle lens can also enhance the look of the sky, especially when there are clouds or northern lights. Try to get close to your foreground and use a small aperture (such as f/11 or f/16) to keep everything in focus.

- Use a tripod. A tripod is essential for photography in Iceland, as it can help you achieve sharp and stable images, especially in low-light situations or when using long exposures. A tripod can also help you compose your shots more carefully and creatively, by allowing you to adjust the angle, height, and orientation of your camera. A tripod can also free your hands from holding the camera, so you can use a remote shutter release or a timer to avoid camera shake. Make sure your tripod is sturdy and stable, and can withstand the wind and the weight of your camera and lens.

- Use filters. Filters are useful accessories for photography in Iceland, as they can help you enhance the colors, contrast, and exposure of your images. There are different types of filters, such as polarizing filters, neutral density filters, and graduated neutral density filters. A polarizing filter can help you reduce reflections and glare from water, ice, or snow, and also increase the saturation and contrast of the sky and the clouds. A neutral density filter can help you reduce the amount of light entering your lens, and allow you to use slower shutter speeds or wider apertures, which can create motion blur or shallow depth of field effects. A graduated neutral density filter can help you balance the exposure between the bright sky and the dark foreground, and avoid overexposing or underexposing parts of your image.

- Use the golden hour and the blue hour. The golden hour and the blue hour are the periods of time around sunrise and sunset, when the light is soft, warm, and colorful. These are the best times for photography in Iceland, as they can create a magical and dramatic atmosphere, and enhance the mood and tone of your images. The golden hour can create a golden glow on the landscape, and the blue hour can create a blue hue on the sky and the water. Try to plan your itinerary and location according to the sunrise and sunset times, and arrive early to scout the best spot and angle. You can also use apps or websites, such as [The Photographer's Ephemeris](^1^) or [SunCalc](^2^), to check the sun position and direction at any time and place.

- Use the rule of thirds. The rule of thirds is a basic composition technique that can help you create balanced and interesting images. The rule of thirds divides your image into nine equal parts, using two horizontal and two vertical lines. The idea is to place the main subject or point of interest at one of the intersections of these lines, or along one of the lines. This can create a sense of movement and dynamism, and also leave some negative space for the viewer's eye to wander. You can also use the rule of thirds to align the horizon with one of the horizontal lines, depending on whether you want to emphasize the sky or the ground. You can use the grid feature on your camera or phone to help you apply the rule of thirds, or you can crop your image later using a photo editing software.

- Experiment with different perspectives. Iceland offers many opportunities to experiment with different perspectives and angles, and create unique and original images. You can try to shoot from a high or low angle, from a close or far distance, from a front or side view, or from a symmetrical or asymmetrical position. You can also use different elements, such as rocks, ice, plants, or animals, to create a foreground, a background, a frame, or a contrast. You can also use different techniques, such as panning, zooming, or tilting, to create a sense of motion, depth, or distortion. The key is to be creative and have fun, and try to capture Iceland from your own point of view.

You can find more information and examples from the web search results that I used to create this response[34]. Have a great day! ●

Source: (1) 100 Best Places for Photographing Iceland + Tips for Aurora (2024). https://www.wedreamoftravel.com/photographing-iceland/.

(2) Iceland Photography Tips for Stunning Travel Photos - Not a Nomad Blog. https://notanomadblog.com/iceland-photography-tips/.

(3) Iceland Photography Tips and Essential Gear for Better Photos. https://www.naturescapes.net/articles/travel/iceland-photography-tips-and-essential-gear-for-better-photos/.

(4) 21 Best Iceland Photography Locations and Tips. https://expertphotography.com/iceland-photography/.

Recommendations for unique souvenirs and local crafts.

Iceland is a country with a rich and diverse culture, history, and nature. There are many unique souvenirs and local crafts that you can buy to remember your trip or to share with your loved ones. Here are some recommendations for the best souvenirs from Iceland:

- Lopapeysa:

This is the iconic Icelandic sweater, made of wool and featuring colorful patterns and designs. The lopapeysa is warm, cozy, and stylish, and can be worn in any season. It is also a symbol of Icelandic identity and tradition, as it is hand-knitted by local artisans. You can find lopapeysas in many shops and markets, such as the Handknitting Association of Iceland[1] or the Kolaportið Flea Market[2]. You can also buy the wool and the patterns and make your own lopapeysa at home.

- Fish skin:

This is a unique and sustainable material that is used to make various products, such as bags, wallets, belts, and jewelry. Fish skin is durable, flexible, and beautiful, and comes in different colors and textures. It is also a way of honoring the fishing heritage of Iceland, as it uses the by-products of the fish industry. You can find fish skin products in many shops and galleries, such as Atlantic Leather[3] or Aurum by Guðbjörg[4].

- Lava stone:

This is a natural and volcanic material that is used to make various products, such as sculptures, jewelry, candles, and soap. Lava stone is black, porous, and lightweight, and has a rough and rustic appearance. It is also a way of celebrating the geology and landscape of Iceland, as it is formed by the eruptions of the volcanoes. You can find lava stone products in many shops and museums, such as Lava Centre[5] or Lava Design[6].

- Icelandic literature: This is a rich and diverse genre that includes novels, poetry, sagas, and children's books. Icelandic literature is known for its creativity, humor, and realism, and reflects the culture and history of Iceland. It is also a way of learning more about the language and the people of Iceland, as it is written in Icelandic or translated into other languages. You can find Icelandic books in many bookstores and libraries, such as Eymundsson or the National Library of Iceland.

- Icelandic chocolate: This is a delicious and high-quality product that is made with local ingredients, such as milk, cream, butter, and berries. Icelandic chocolate is smooth, creamy, and flavorful, and comes in different varieties and shapes. It is also a way of indulging in the sweetness and freshness of Iceland, as it is produced by local chocolatiers. You can find Icelandic chocolate in many shops and cafes, such as Omnom Chocolate or Kaffitár.

These are some of the best souvenirs from Iceland that you can buy to remember your trip or to share with your loved ones. They are unique, authentic, and meaningful, and represent the culture, history, and nature of Iceland. I hope this helps you write elaborately on recommendations for unique souvenirs and local crafts in Iceland. Have a great day! ●

Source:
(1) The Top 11 Souvenirs From Iceland | Guide to Iceland.
https://guidetoiceland.is/best-of-iceland/top-10-souvenirs-from-iceland.

(2) 15 Best Iceland Gifts and Souvenirs You Will Love.
https://icelandtrippers.com/best-iceland-gifts-and-souvenirs/.

(3) The best souvenirs from Iceland.
https://bing.com/search?q=Recommendations+for+unique+souvenirs+and+local+crafts+in+Iceland.

(4) The best souvenirs from Iceland.
https://www.visiticeland.com/article/the-best-souve
nirs-from-iceland/.

(5) Are there any traditional crafts or souvenirs unique to Iceland?.
https://www.adequatetravel.com/info/iceland/are-th
ere-any-traditional-crafts-or-souvenirs-unique-to-ice
land.

(6) 15 Souvenirs To Bring Back From Iceland: To Remember Forever!.
https://pickyourtrail.com/blog/15-souvenirs-from-ic
eland/.

Acknowledgment

"I would like to express my heartfelt gratitude to all the individuals, businesses, and organizations in Iceland who generously shared their insights, knowledge, and hospitality. This travel guide would not have been possible without their support and the unique experiences they provided. I extend my appreciation to the diverse and welcoming people of Iceland, who make this city a remarkable destination. Thank you for opening the doors to your culture and city, and for making every visitor feel at home."

Who can check more of my books?
France Revealed
Barcelona: A guide for all Seasons and many more.

God bless.

Printed in Great Britain
by Amazon

37634998R00096